The Book of
Princetown

Thomas Tyrwhitt's Dartmoor Town

Christopher Gardner-Thorpe

HALSGROVE

First published in Great Britain in 2003

British Library Cataloguing-in-Publication Data
A CIP record for this title is available from the British Library

ISBN 1 84114 239 5

HALSGROVE

Halsgrove House
Lower Moor Way
Tiverton, Devon EX16 6SS
Tel: 01884 243242
Fax: 01884 243325
email: sales@halsgrove.com
website: www.halsgrove.com

Frontispiece photograph: *In the prison quarry.* (FO)

Printed and bound in Great Britain by CPI Bath Press, Bath.

FOREWORD

The Duchy of Cornwall has been intimately involved with Princetown from its foundation. Dartmoor itself is part of the original history of the Duchy. In 1239 Henry III granted the Forest of Dartmoor to Richard, Earl of Cornwall, and 98 years later, in 1337, it passed into the hands of the Black Prince as part of the Duchy of Cornwall when he was created the first Duke.

Many of us in the Duchy of Cornwall have a strong attachment to the moor, both as a place to work but also where we have enjoyed its remoteness, environment and wonderful scenery. It is, however, the people who live on the moor and what they have done there that has created its history and made it what it is today.

The particular pleasure for me in writing this foreword for *The Book of Princetown* is that, as the first chapter explains, it was a previous Secretary of the Council of the Duchy of Cornwall, Thomas Tyrwhitt, who had an ambitious plan in 1795 to tame the moorland from which the origins of the village were created. The beginning appears to lie with the creation of Tor Royal Farm, cottages and the construction of the Plume of Feathers public house. Even today these buildings remain part of the Duchy's estate. Sir Thomas' entrepreneurial spirit is pronounced most visibly in the scale of the prison, and it was this complex of buildings that led to the logic of much of the building activity that followed.

Past reliance on such a dominant influence on the village's development inevitably leads to challenges for the community that has evolved. I find that in many ways the Duchy of Cornwall still has an empathy with the way that Thomas Tyrwhitt felt 200 years ago, of wanting to help progress.

This book is described as a history about and for the local community. The present Duke of Cornwall, His Royal Highness The Prince of Wales, still attaches the highest importance to local communities and everything that they mean to the evolution of this country and its culture, and which he emphasises through both the Duchy of Cornwall and other organisations, including The Prince's Trust and Business in the Community, of which he is president.

The long history of Princetown, which is so well illustrated in this book, is something that we are proud to share. We are committed to continue playing our part in the future success and strength of the village and its

community. This may not be on such an ambitious scale as my predecessor but, with its remoteness and the hardiness of the environment, it is certain that the community today is built on solid foundations – like the granite on which the village stands.

Bertie Ross
Secretary and Keeper of the Records
Duchy of Cornwall
15th September 2003

Left: 'Uncle' Ernie Worth delivering milk in the snow with horse and cart outside Hessary Terrace. (DG)

3

A photograph of Dartmoor, near Princetown.

Right: *Two bungalows seen across the moor from the Yelverton to Princetown road in the snows of January 1963.* (GD)

Mount Edgecumb's gatepost at Merrivale Quarry. (IM)

Trees on Tavistock Road hide the prison water tower on the right. (RJ)

CONTENTS

Left: *A convict with horse and cart, 1908.* (RJ)

Below: *Ponies in Princetown Square, looking south.* (FO)

Below: *Looking south down Tavistock Road with Hessary Terrace and the school in the distance on the left.* (AG)

Prisoners outside the old Police Station on Tavistock Road looking north. The church tower can just be seen over the rooftops of the houses on the left. On the right is the Imperial Hotel which later became the Post Office and was subsequently demolished. (DG)

ACKNOWLEDGEMENTS

Many new friends have been most generous with information, encouragement and the loan of images. Initials identify those who have kindly provided the images. The author is deeply indebted to each and hopes that he has not made too many errors of omission and commission. Where the identity of a person in a photograph is not known, the caption bears a question mark. Without the help of all who have lent photographs and memories, this project would not have been possible.

Amongst those who have helped are: Shirley Agness (SA), Peter Bolt, Sue Bolt, Louis Brown (LB), Sheila Coates, George Cole (GC), Brian and Brenda Cooper (BC), Clarence Cooper, David Cooper (DC), Winnie Cooper, Hector and Mabel Cribbett (HC), Les and Evelyn Cribbett (LC), Allan and Mabel Cross (AC), Peter Crozier (PC), Eric Cruse, Greta Doble (GD), Ralph and Chris Eriksson (RE), Alasdair Forbes (AF), Rene Frampton (RF), David German (DG), Eric Green, Karen and Gordon Green, Ann and Peter Grigg (AG), the late Bernard Hext (BH), Ron Joy (RJ), George Langton (GL), James Langton, Bob Law, Carole McAuliffe, Ivan Mead (IM), Reverend Robert Ormsby (RRO), Margery Ousley (MO), Fred and Mandy Owen (FO), Rosie Oxenham (RO), Gael Phillips, Bill Radcliffe, Dennis and Becky Reece (DBR), Louis Rich (LR), Derek Roper (DR), William Short (WS), Arthur Smith (AS), David Sones, Heather and Ted Stanley (TS), Les and Chris Stephens (LS), John and Wendy Stones (JS), David Swales, Malcolm and Rosalind Waite, Ken and Hilda Watson, John Waycott (JW), Freda Wilkinson (FW), Gladys Williams and Don Youngson (DY). Colin Sturmer, formerly of the Duchy Office in Princetown, was generous and helpful with his time.

Naomi Cudmore, Simon Butler and others at Halsgrove have handled the images and text with great sensitivity and tolerance which has enhanced immensely the author's enjoyment of this special project. Sadie Butler has designed the book with patience and, with Naomi, she deserves special thanks.

Two Bridges Road looking west. **(FO)**

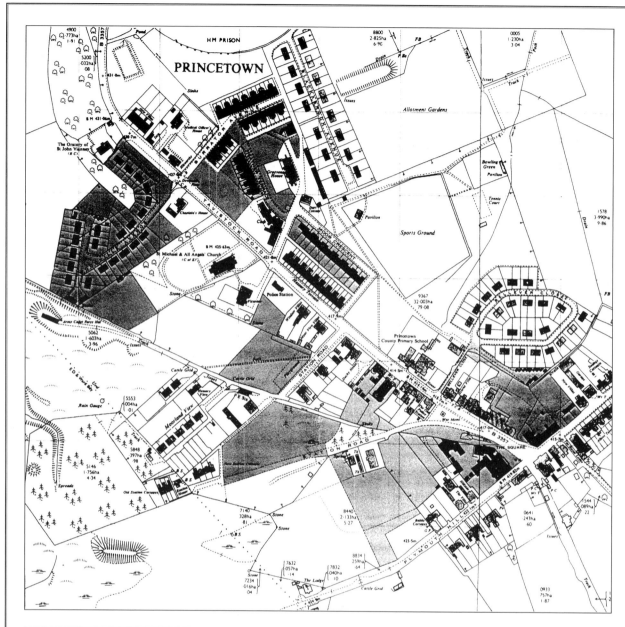

Above: *A map of Princetown, mid-1900s.* (RO)

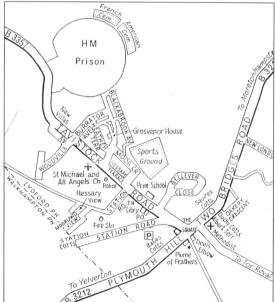

Left: *A plan of Princetown, late 1900s.* (JS)

The Plume of Feathers in Princetown Square. (RJ)

INTRODUCTION

When Princetown is mentioned, many think first of the prison and of the cold, wet air of Dartmoor. Princetown is 1,400 feet above sea level, the highest town in England. Indeed, nothing of significant height is interposed between Princetown and the land across the Atlantic, towards both Newfoundland and the Falklands. The Falklands have been described as 'Dartmoor at high tide'.[1] Of Princetown, the Reverend Sabine Baring-Gould wrote: 'The situation is particularly exposed and injudiciously chosen on a col, where every mist and cloud catches and clings, and without any shelter whatever.'[2]

Much of the town is intricately bound up with the prison and those who work in it, and the layout and buildings have mostly evolved from the prison and its community. The area around the town is owned largely by the Duchy of Cornwall and the Home Office is the major tenant, although the National Park Authority has played a greater part in recent years. Before the control of prisons fell under the auspices of the Home Office, Princetown was a garrison town where soldiers were stationed to keep the peace.

Princetown already features in many of the classic works on Dartmoor; the present volume does not pretend to be an academic tome on the subject, but instead is a history about and for the local community. It is not surprising therefore that much of the content is parochial. Care has been taken to avoid, as far as possible, inclusion of images and significant text that may be seen elsewhere, and readers may wish to examine other volumes to complete the picture provided here. Special care has been taken to obtain first-hand information from living persons and old documents.

The Community History Series, published by Halsgrove of Tiverton, includes an impressive array of villages and towns throughout Devon and beyond. Each volume in the series is unique, every community deciding how to present their studies. *The Book of Princetown* is based largely on pictorial history and is laid out as if the reader were setting off on a journey from Princetown Square. In each chapter buildings and walls will be considered to the left of the walker on the outward journey and again on the return. Community Histories draw on information from many sources, essentially those whose roots, ancient or modern, lie in the neighbourhood. Childhood memories abound among those still living in Princetown and others who have moved away.[3] William Crossing (1847–1928) is perhaps the best-known writer on Dartmoor. Of the many books about the region,[4] several deal specifically with Princetown and the surrounding area.[5] The author acknowledges with gratitude the information provided by the writers of these volumes. Reference to periodicals about Dartmoor are rewarding too.[6] Images are important and the paintings of William Widgery (1826–93) and F.J. Widgery have entranced over the ages.[7]

Notes
1. Thanks to John Stones who related this fact after a trip to the Falklands.
2. Baring-Gould, S., *Devon*, Methuen, London, 1907, p.253.
3. Richardson, D., 'Dartmoor Memories: A Schoolboy in Princetown', in *Dartmoor News 61* and *62*, 2001, pp41–42 and 32–34.
4. Baring-Gould, S., *A Book of Dartmoor*, Methuen, 1900; Brewer, D., *A Field Guide to the Boundary Markers On and Around Dartmoor*, Devon Books, 1986; Hemery, E., *High Dartmoor, Land and People*, Robert Hale, London, 1983.
5. Barber, C., *Princetown of Yesteryear, Parts I and II*, Obelisk Publications, Exeter; Crossing, W., *Princetown, Its Rise and Progress*, Quay Publications, Brixham, 1989; James, T., *About Princetown*, Orchard Publications, Chudleigh, 2002.
6. *Dartmoor Magazine*, Quay Publications; *Dartmoor, the Country Magazine*, Halsgrove; *Dartmoor News*, Okehampton; *The Dartmoor Society Newsletter*, Tavistock.
7. Baker, C.J., 'William Widgery 1826–93', in *Dartmoor Magazine 30*, 1993, pp6–8; Stephens-Hodge, M., 'Dartmoor Through the Eyes of the Widgerys', in *Dartmoor Magazine 67*, 2002, pp22–23.

Princetown from the south. (RJ)

Eight bullocks were killed by lightning at Princetown on 4 September 1913. (FO)

ONE

ᘛᘉᘀᘉᘃ

WHERE IS PRINCETOWN?

Princetown, the highest town in England and the western entry point for Dartmoor, is a wet and windy place with an average annual rainfall of 82 inches. Some 375 million years ago Devonian limestone was laid down in the warm, shallow seas.[1] Through this solid rock, 280 million years ago, Dartmoor's granite – molten and laden with minerals – was forced up through the limestone to form the granite masses and mineral veins which create part of the band that extends through Cornwall and emerges on Bodmin Moor, in the Isles of Scilly and out at sea. One-and-a-half million years ago the first of a series of ice ages began, during which glaciers extended south as far as Bristol. Underwater caves were formed half a million years ago. Before the sea levels rose and when continental Europe and Britain were one land mass, the River Dart was a tributary of the river we now call the Rhine.

On Dartmoor, where permanent habitation began some 4,000 years ago, building materials from the earliest hut circles and other structures were probably reused to construct walls and homesteads during the twelfth and thirteenth centuries. The Duchy Review of 1357 produced a list of local tenements, one of which, Prince Hall, survives with the same name today. In 1772, when the road from Two Bridges to Moretonhampstead was started, Judge Buller of Prince Hall built cottages at Two Bridges and an inn, the Saracen's Head.[2] Granite continued to be used through the centuries and its popularity increased during the 1800s. Indeed, Princetown's survival is due in large part to the presence of the massive granite workings nearby.

Also, of course, the town has thrived as a result of its proximity to Dartmoor Prison, formerly known as Dartmoor Convict Prison, and through tourism.

Princetown from the west. (RJ)

Prince Hall from a watercolour by John Swete, 1797. (DG)

John Cooper (formerly of Nun's Cross Farm) outside Prince Hall Farm. (DG)

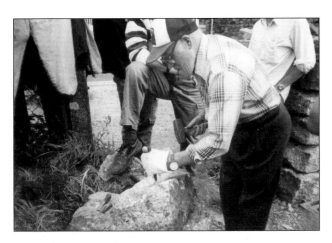

Clifford Waycott shows students how to split granite behind The Prince of Wales pub, 1980s. (JW)

The North Hessary Tor transmitter, a stark landmark, provides employment for a few, but many residents are associated in some capacity with the prison and its activities.

Princetown as we know it today owes its beginnings to Thomas Tyrwhitt (1762–1833), born the son of an Essex vicar in 1762.[3] After completing his MA at Christ Church College, Oxford, he became friend and Private Secretary to George Augustus Frederick (1762–1830), the Prince of Wales (the future King George IV), who was also the Duke of Cornwall.[4] In 1785 Tyrwhitt built the Prince's Arms (presumably named in honour of his friend but now known as the Plume of Feathers) and several cottages. A decade later he also built a home for himself, at Tor Royal, and, the following year, was appointed Auditor to the Duchy of Cornwall. Tyrwhitt dreamed of opening up Dartmoor, making it more accessible to people from the surrounding towns, especially Plymouth, and at the same time of turning a vast stretch of wild moor into a productive agricultural district.

In 1798 Tyrwhitt developed his 2,300-acre Tor Royal estate where it was his ambition to build up a small community that in time would become virtually self-sufficient. Originally he intended the development to be centred around the Two Bridges area, and he improved the road from there to Dousland and also formed a new highway leading from the lodges of his estate to Rundlestone, with a gate at each end of it. In the spirit of the times, the lower one, Barrack Gate, was a toll-gate. To the new, and still tiny, settlement Tyrwhitt gave the name Prince's Town (or Princetown as it became known).[5] Rumour has it that the Prince himself did visit Tor Royal at some point, but others maintain that his only trip to Devon was to see his brother, the Duke of Clarence, off from Plymouth.

In 1803 (by which time Tyrwhitt had been appointed Warden of the Stannaries), Britain and France commenced war once again. French prisoners of war were detained in the hulks of old ships moored in Plymouth Sound and from time to time were transferred to prisons at Plymouth, Peterborough and Bristol. However, overcrowding was a problem and a new prison was required to house these men. In 1805, the year of the Battle of Trafalgar, Tyrwhitt recommended Prince's Town to the Government as a suitable site. On 20 July Daniel Alexander, the esteemed architect, met an official of the Board of Transport at Tor Royal and the suggestion was adopted. Tyrwhitt wanted a chapel to be included in the new prison but this did not materialise for a further five years.

In January 1806, through his Duchy of Cornwall office, the Prince Regent granted 390 acres in the Forest of Dartmoor on a 99-year lease for the building of a prison, and on 20 March Tyrwhitt laid the foundation-stone. The prison had been completed by 1808 at a cost of £127,000. Cottages for the prison staff were also built and on 24 May 1809 some 2,500 prisoners of war were marched up from Plymouth where they had been incarcerated. By 30 June there were 5,000 prisoners on the prison roll. A mill and bakery were set up at Bachelor's Hall and a brewery established behind the officers' hostel. The beginnings of the prison farm were also by this time in existence where Tyrwhitt had enclosed land around Tor Royal and erected farm buildings. (The land was suitable for arable farming and he grew flax – with no little degree of success, apparently, as the Bath and West Agricultural Society awarded him a medal.).

The War of 1812 against the United States began in June of that year and the French prisoners of war at Princetown were now joined by their American naval counterparts. Together they were employed – for 6d. a day – to build a chapel for the prison which is now known as St Michael's Church and which was first used for divine worship (in its uncompleted form) in March 1814. The growing volume of commerce at Princetown demanded a good turnpike cart road to Plymouth and cemeteries also had to be built for the prisoners. In recognition of his dedicated works at Princetown Tyrwhitt was knighted and appointed 'Usher of Black Rod'. It would not be long, however, before Princetown was deserted once again; the French and American prisoners departed the war prison in 1815–16, and peace returned to the town almost as quickly as it had been shattered.

By 1818 Tyrwhitt's increasingly busy granite quarries in Walkhampton required a tramroad to Crabtree Wharf on the Plym estuary from whence a growing volume of granite was to be shipped. Work began in 1819 and by 1820 the tramroad had been extended from Crabtree to Sutton Pool in Plymouth. It was to be called the Plymouth & Dartmoor Railway and it finally opened in September 1823 (although not complete). Constructed of iron rails bolted to granite blocks and with granite sidings, the horse tramway, the first iron railroad in Devon, was completed in December of 1825 and two years later

Left: *The arrival of the Prince and Princess of Wales at the Duchy Hotel, Princetown, 10 June 1909.* (FO)

prison). During the second half of the nineteenth century the growth of the prison led to prosperity in Princetown, the prison farmlands were developed and the Duchy Hotel, which served, in part, as accommodation for the prison officers, flourished.

In 1859 the South Devon & Tavistock Railway was opened, running from Plymouth to Tavistock, in 1877 a steam-operated railway to Plymouth was discussed and in 1879 the Plymouth & Dartmoor Railway Company was formed at Paddington. Three years later, in 1882, work started on the permanent way on Tyrwhitt's old track and on 11 August 1883 a new station was built at Hessary Col, with a road to the village called Frenchmen's Row.

From Yelverton the train climbed for nine-and-a-half of the ten-and-a-half miles of track, negotiating sharp curves but enjoying panoramic views over Dartmoor.

The railways expanded during the twentieth century before the First World War and animals were brought up the Princetown line to central Dartmoor. On 10 June 1909 the Prince and Princess of Wales arrived at Tavistock Station and travelled by car to Princetown where the Duchy Hotel had recently been renovated.

After 1918 the changing economy led to the vacating of many farms. During the Second World War the War Office requisitioned much of Dartmoor for military training and this had a major impact on agriculture. Tourism by car increased and the local railway lost money, eventually closing in March 1956. This was the beginning of a period of major change in Princetown.

was extended north from the quarries to Princetown, a total distance of 25 miles from Sutton Pool. It crossed the turnpike road between Princetown and Rundlestone and terminated at the Devil's Elbow Hotel at a point christened 'the wharf' – a relic of the term formerly used for the terminus of horse-drawn barges on the canals. Later this terminus became the village store and the hotel was renamed The Railway Inn. By 1830, with the demand for Dartmoor granite growing and output increasing, the railroad (which was also being used on the upward journey to bring stores and coal to Princetown) had become even more valuable for the Walkham Quarries; the granite was especially popular with architects of some of the grandest public buildings and monuments in the nation's capital – Buckingham Palace, Nelson's Column, Vauxhall Bridge and New Scotland Yard to name but a few.

In 1833 Tyrwhitt undertook a diplomatic errand to France and on 24 February of that year he died, in Calais. It would not be long before another era was to draw to a close in Princetown. The granite from Foggintor, Swell Tor and King's Tor was deemed to be inferior to that from Haytor, lying some miles east of Princetown, and by about 1840 the granite industry in the immediate environs of the town was declining. Princetown's population became further depleted as a result.

In 1846 the British Patent Naphtha Company moved its peat works from Bachelor's Hall to the prison building and a new tramroad was built at a cost of £19,000 to service the facility. However, the naphtha produced at Princetown, being excessively smokey, did not sell well and the company quickly went bankrupt. The works closed in 1849.

In the meantime, convict prisons across the country were becoming desperately overcrowded as fewer and fewer convicts were transported to the colonies. Extra accommodation had to be found for these prisoners on home shores and a decision was made to turn Dartmoor Prison into a convict settlement. The first convicts arrived on 2 November 1850. In 1854 civil guards replaced the military guards (a hangover from the era of the war

Notes

1. Hallet, J., *Around Princetown's Quarries*, Orchard Publications, Chudleigh, 1994; Brewer, K., *The Railways, Quarries and Cottages of Foggintor*, Orchard Publications, Chudleigh, 1999.
2. Brewer, D., 'Judge Sir Francis Buller and Dartmoor', in *Dartmoor Magazine 35*, 1994, pp22–23.
3. Landon, L., 'Sir Thomas Tyrwhitt, His Life and Times', in *Dartmoor Magazine 15*, 1989, pp4–6; Rendell, P., 'Great Dartmoor Folks: Tyrwhitt and Alexander, The Men Who Built Princetown', in *Dartmoor News 66*, 2002, pp23–25.
4. Palmer, A., *The Life and Times of George IV*, Weidenfeld and Nicolson, London, 1972.
5. Cocks, John Somers, 'Exploitation', in Gill, C., *Dartmoor: A New Study*, David & Charles, Newton Abbot, 1977, p.251.

TWO

THE ROAD TO THE NORTH: TAVISTOCK ROAD

Tavistock Road, Princetown. (RO)

The road to the north of Princetown Square is the old road from the Plume of Feathers to Rundlestone. It was first named Tyrwhitt Road and later Prison Road before becoming Tavistock Road.

The building that would later become the **Duchy Hotel** (it was converted by James Rowe during the 1850s) was constructed in 1809 to provide bachelor accommodation, and a brewery, for the Army officers at the prison (although junior ranks lived at the barracks). More than a century later, history would repeat itself when the hotel began, in 1941, to be used as an officers' mess. This continued until 1991 and the building later became the High Moorland Visitor Centre. In 2003 it houses the Duchy Office (the Duchy has had an office in Princetown since 1934)

and other offices, as well as a fine exhibition of Dartmoor life.

The Duke and Duchess (then Mrs Simpson) of Windsor based themselves at the Duchy Hotel for riding at Tor Royal and Peat Cot, while Eden Phillpotts, who wrote historical fiction based on Dartmoor, as well as Sir Arthur Conan Doyle, author of *The Hound of the Baskervilles*, also stayed here.[1]

Outside the Duchy Hotel is the **Jubilee Lamp** of 1887, erected to commemorate the silver jubilee of Queen Victoria 50 years after the accession in 1837. Celebrations on this occasion in the town included a meat tea and a bonfire on North Hessary Tor.[2] Oil- and gas-lamps lit Princetown until 1947 when electricity arrived. On Princetown Village Green a

Dartmoor ponies and bus outside the Duchy Hotel in Princetown Square. **(FO)**

Above: *Hessary Terrace, Tavistock Road, 2002. It was formerly G block for prison officers (1908).*

Right: *The view from Princetown Village Green.*

Princetown Square, looking north, with the Jubilee Lamp on the left. **(JW)**

Left: *Dartmoor Prison Bowls Club versus Mount Gould on the prison bowling-green.* (DG)

Below: *A letter sent to 'Mrs Turnpike and others', from Buckingham Palace, 26 February 1872. 'Major General Sir J.M. Biddulph is commanded by the Queen to acknowledge the address of the invalid inmates of the Royal Hospital for Incurables, in which they offer to Her Majesty, and to the Prince of Wales, their congratulations on the recovery of the Prince. Her Majesty fully appreciates the kind feeling which prompts them and receives, with more than ordinary gratification, the good of those whom it has pleased Providence to afflict and, in their affliction, so warmly participate in the general joy and thankfulness to God for his mercy to the Queen and the nation.'*

Left: *Tim Easterbrook (left) in the snow, 1963.* (SA)

Above: *Before the snow was cleared, 1963.* (SA)

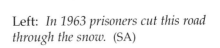

Left: *In 1963 prisoners cut this road through the snow.* (SA)

Left: *During the winter of 1963 the snow piled up in Tavistock Road. Princetown Square is on the extreme left.* (SA)

Below and below left: *Princetown Square, 1963. Much of the snow was taken on to the moor by lorry.* (SA)

Above: *The Plume of Feathers and the Duchy Hotel, 1963.* (SA)

Above right: *Station Road junction and the school, 1963.* (SA)

Right: *The Square in 1963.* (SA)

Left: *The prison houses, 1963. On top of the snow are Leslie Mutton (right) and his wife, Winnie. Stan Wanless, Industrial Manager at the prison, stands on the road.* (SA)

Below: *Clearing snow, 1963.* (SA)

Mrs Clyst feeding the sheep with crusts of bread. **(SA)**

Right: *The snow in 1963.* (SA)

Clearing the deep snow in Two Bridges Road, 1963. **(SA)**

Above: *The Duchy Hotel on the left and, on the right, Caunter's Row, which subsequently became Lord's Café.* (DG)

Right: *The Duchy Hotel, c.1885.* (DG)

Hunt meet outside the Duchy Hotel. (DG)

Buses parked outside the Duchy Hotel, Princetown. The Devil's Elbow can be seen in the distance and Lord's Café is situated on the left, c.1950s. (DG)

Above: *A card showing two interior views of the Duchy Hotel and another with the hunt outside at the time when Aaron Rowe was proprietor.*

Above left: *Licence 323 granted to James Julian Duncan Rowe, dated 11 October 1852, to retail spirits at the Duchy Hotel.*

Left: *The Duchy Hotel before the stone exterior was rebuilt and extended in Edwardian style in 1909.* (ALL DG)

Right: *The dining-room in the Prison Officers' Mess at the Duchy Hotel, early 1970s.* (RJ)

Below: *The lounge in the Prison Officers' Mess at the Duchy Hotel, early 1970s.* (RJ)

Princetown, Devon.—Highly Valuable Leasehold Hotel and Land Adjoining.

THURSDAY, JUNE 9th, 1898.

SKARDON, SONS & HOSKING

Are favoured with instructions from the Owner, to SELL BY AUCTION at their

Commercial Sale Rooms, Cornwall St., Plymouth,

On Thursday, June 9th, 1898, at **4** o'clock,

(Subject to the general conditions of the Incorporated Law Society of Plymouth, and such special conditions as shall then be read) all that VALUABLE & IMPROVING

PROPERTY

KNOWN AS THE:

DUCHY HOTEL

PRINCETOWN,

Now and for many years past in the occupation of Mr. Aaron Rowe.

It contains on the Ground floor, Good Bar, Two Sitting Rooms, large Dining Room, Private Room, Tap-room, Dairy, Lavatory and Laundry, Kitchen, and Boot house. There is excellent cellarage in the basement. On the First floor are Ten Bedrooms and Two w.c.'s. In rear is a large stable yard, with extensive and conveniently arranged Stabling and Coach-houses, Piggeries, Poultry-house.

With the above will be sold

5 FIELDS or Closes of Land,

Immediately adjoining, containing by admeasurement 15a. 2r. 37p., or thereabouts.

The Property is well situate, and is probably the best known and most frequented Hotel within many miles of this popular health resort, and is let to Mr. Rowe on lease, at a yearly rent of £71, the tenant paying all Rates and Taxes, including land tax and tithe-rent charge, and is held from the Duchy of Cornwall until Michaelmas, 1907, at a ground rent of £3 2s. 7d., and an audit fee of 3s. 4d.

May be viewed at any time, and further particulars had of the Auctioneers ; or of

Messrs. SKARDON & PHILLIPS, Solicitors,

VICTORIA CHAMBERS, PLYMOUTH.

PRINTED BY HOYTEN & COLE, 11, RUSSELL STREET, PLYMOUTH.

Above: *An advertisement for the sale of the Duchy Hotel on 9 June 1898.* (DG)

Above: *The Duchy Hotel, after rebuilding.* (FO)

Right: *Princetown Square and the Duchy Hotel (left).* (FO)

Right: *The hunt in Princetown Square with the Devil's Elbow in the background* (left) *and the Plume of Feathers* (right). (JW)

Above: *Ponies outside Lord's Cafe.* (FO)

Below: *The Square, Princetown, with Bolt's Store* (left) *and The Railway Hotel* (right). *Bowden's Café is to the left of the Hotel.* (RO)

Ponies in Princetown Square. This photograph was taken before frequent accidents led to a decision to install cattle (pony) grids. (JW)

Above: *Agricultural market in Princetown, 1900.* (LB)

Right: *Ponies near Princetown War Memorial, looking south.* (FO)

Dartmoor ponies in Princetown Square, 1948. The photograph includes: *Margaret Cribbett, Janet Morgan, Ann Grigg, Heather Warne* (front) *and Billy Fielder* (back). (AG)

Left: *The Dartmoor National Park information caravan arrived at Princetown on 10 May 1965 at a cost of £800.* (DG)

Right: *Sir Henry Slesser at the opening of the Dartmoor Information Centre at Princetown on Monday 10 May 1965. The event was reported in The Times, 14 May 1965.* (DG)

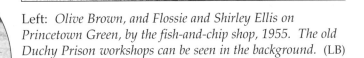

Left: *Olive Brown, and Flossie and Shirley Ellis on Princetown Green, by the fish-and-chip shop, 1955. The old Duchy Prison workshops can be seen in the background.* (LB)

Below: *The dedication of the War Memorial on Princetown Village Green.*

The War Memorial on Princetown Village Green, 2003.

Above: *Princetown War Memorial, 2002.*

Above left: *Two Dartmoor ponies grazing near the War Memorial in Duchy Square.* (DG)

Below: *The old Fire Station.* (FO)

Above, below and bottom right: *Three Princetown fire engines.* (FO)

At the old Fire Station with (left to right) *Percy Cooper, Bill Roper and Bert Horwell.* (DC)

large tree was lost in a hurricane in 1987 and was replaced in 2002 as part of the silver jubilee celebrations for Queen Elizabeth II.

The **Village Green** and **War Memorial** provide an area of grass on the left. Before the cattle grids were installed, Dartmoor ponies used to roam the streets and the Square, occasionally eating the bread carried under the arms of unsuspecting pedestrians but generally delighting the visitors.

The road to Station Cottages runs to the west, to the site of the old railway station, following the path of the railway line[3 & 4] that ran south-east to its terminus at the Devil's Elbow. The railway boundary markers were the perfect height for standing on while mounting a pushbike; two of these, which can be seen on the Village Green, bear the inscription 'Great Western Railway Co. Boundary 1895'. The entrance to **Royal Court** is on this road *(see page 51)*.

Further down this road on the left-hand side is a badge factory, 'Pressed Men', in a building that was once the Power Station and later the Masonic Hall. Beyond stands the **Fire Station**, built on the defunct carriage sidings and the horse-drawn railway. The stable block is the only remaining part of the original station, although there is a reminder of it in the naming of the row of houses, **Station Cottages,** bordering the right-hand side of the site to the north. Railway

Cottages included, to the west, a row of three houses – for the driver, the packer and the guard – and a single house to the east for the stationmaster.

In 1883 the steam railway[5] was introduced to Princetown via a branch line from Yelverton where the track then joined the main line to Plymouth. The railway was used to transport supplies to Princetown as well as to take away products manufactured by the prisoners, including handcarts, cartwheels, wheelbarrows, mailbags and coal sacks. On one occasion a stack of ex-Army wooden trestle tables arrived in Princetown; the metal hinges were removed from each table and the wood was recycled. Coal was imported and used for the gasworks at the prison and prison staff were able to buy the residual coke cheaply.

The trains also carried passengers; football fans paying 2s.6d. for the 'Saturday Special' at Plymouth Argyle Football Ground, cinema-goers, and pupils travelling to Tavistock School. On release, prisoners were escorted to the railway station with suit, trilby hat and suitcase and would leave Princetown with a railway warrant (some to return in due course).

Sometimes youngsters alighted at King's Tor Halt and ran downhill to meet the train at Ingra Tor; when they were too slow the train would arrive first and wait for the breathless passengers to rejoin. Ingra was the station for Criptor Quarry and local residents would have to carry their heavy shopping across the moor here. On one occasion the train driver lost his false teeth and had to stop the train to retrieve them – passengers helped in the search.

Princetown Fair[6] was held annually on the first Wednesday of September in the old **Cattle Market**, next to the station car park. Gypsies would sell items such as clothes pegs, and fish and chips were served. Many private roads in the area needed to be closed for one day each year in order to preserve their private status and Fair Day was an ideal opportunity to do this as blocking off the roads (with which the prison officers lent a hand) helped to prevent the animals from straying.

Princetown's old Police Station is home to a fish-and-chip café, beyond which stand the **Post**

(continues page 43)

A boundary marker for Great Western Railway land.

Princetown Cattle Market, late 1940s. (LC)

27

Princetown Railway Station with a terrace of three houses (left) for the staff, a detached house for the stationmaster, the engine-house, and the site of the Cattle Market (back right) with the church in the background, early 1900s. (BC)

Above left:
Princetown GWR Station. (RJ)

Above and left:
Two views of the disused stable which once housed the animals used on the horse-drawn railway, 2003.

Above: *An aerial view of Princetown Station showing the layout of the railway lines and sidings. The prison is just outside the picture area* (left). *On the right are the two lodges at the entrance to Princetown on Plymouth Road.* (DG)

Above: *Locomotive 4410 at Burrator and Sheepstor on its way up to Princetown, 1955.* (DG)

Right: *A train near the skyline to the left of the picture proceeds towards Princetown, 1955. Ingra Tor Station is in the foreground.* (DG)

Left: *Care-free camping in comfort, 1934. A corner of the dining-room in the GWR camp coach for six people, with two-berth sleeping compartments. Some 19 camp coaches were available during the 1934 holiday season – one in Somerset, six in Devon, three in Cornwall and nine in Wales. Princetown was one site, the highest point on the GWR at 1,373 feet above sea level.* (DG)

Below: *Locomotive 4410, a 2-6-2T at Yelverton, on 5 July 1955.* (DG)

A train enters Horrabridge Station. (DG)

Below: *Yelverton Station was opened in 1885. The line operated by GWR opened in 1883 and the distance between Yelverton and Princetown was ten-and-a-half miles, climbing 950 feet. The trip up took 41 minutes and the journey down 30 minutes. The last train travelled in September 1955 and the line was closed in March 1956. This photograph was taken in the early 1900s.* (DG)

Above: *A train heading for Yelverton emerging from the tunnel on the line to Horrabridge.* (DG)

Above: *A train on its way to Princetown, 1953. Sharpitor radio mast can be seen on the skyline. One of many masts erected around the country for radar navigation, it was built of wood and used by the Royal Observer Corps for aeroplane identification training.* (DG)

Right: *The railway bridge at Peek Hill, c.1950. The bridge has since been demolished although the abutments remain.* (DG)

The blizzard of March 1891. (DG)

Right: *A blizzard at the Eggworthy cutting, March 1891. Note the tall smoke stack, the expansion chamber for the boiler tubes on the engine and the clerestory coach.* (DG)

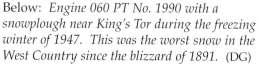

Left: *In December 1927 engine 060 PT was fitted with a snowplough helped by engine 44XX.* (DG)

Below: *Engine 060 PT No. 1990 with a snowplough near King's Tor during the freezing winter of 1947. This was the worst snow in the West Country since the blizzard of 1891.* (DG)

Left: *Navy personnel helping locomotive 060 PT No. 1990, 1947.* (DG)

Above: *A view of Princetown looking south-east across the railway, with the church on the left.* (DG)

Left: *Wilfred Hext, porter on the Princetown Railway.* (LS)

Above: *A train bound for Princetown travels around the King's Tor loop below the tor itself.* (DG)

Left: *Princetown from the moor. Note the road bridge on the way into Princetown.* (DG)

Left: *Engine 4408, 1951. The fireman* (in the cab) *was C. Stephens. Left to right: R. Eden, F. Prowse, Charlie Windsor (stationmaster), J. Hannaford.* (DG)

Below: *A wartime group at Princetown Station, 1941. At this time some of the men had gone to war and women staffed the station. Left to right, back row: A. Stephens (porter), S. Rendle (platform guard), S. Brokenshire (signalman); front: Joan Stephens (wartime porter), C. Windsor (stationmaster), Joan Stacey (stationmaster's assistant).* (DG)

Above: *Princetown Station from the south, c.1910. Note the church in the centre of the picture.* (DG)

Below: *A goat and a passenger pose for the camera at Princetown Station.* (DG)

BR(WR) Working Timetable. Period 20th Sep. 1954 — 12th Jun. 1955.

WEEKDAYS — YELVERTON AND PRINCETOWN

SINGLE LINE, worked by Electric Train Staff. No intermediate Crossing place.

Mile Post Mileage		Mileage from Yelverton		DOWN	Ruling Gradient 1 in	B Mixed	B Mixed	B Mixed
							SX	SO
M	C	M	C			am	PM	PM
0	0	—	—	YELVERTON.......... dep	—	9 4	2 28	2 52
1	47	1	47	Dousland...	40 R	9 10	2 35	2 58
2	72	2	72	Burrator Halt	40 R	9 16	2 41	3 4
6	20	6	20	Ingra Tor Halt	42 F	9 28	2 53	3 16
8	74	8	74	King Tor Halt	55 R	9 39	3 4	3 27
10	43	10	43	PRINCETOWN ... arr	47 R	9 45	3 10	3 33

British Rail (Western Region) working timetable for the period 20 September 1954 until 12 June 1955. Note the two trains per day whose speed was not to exceed 20 miles per hour. (DG)

The Princetown Express, 1955. (HC)

Below: *A tank engine entering Princetown Station, 1926. (DG)*

Below: *In steam at Princetown Station, 1955. (DG)*

Below left: *Engine 4410 with carriage. (DG)*

Above: *A nasty smash-up on the moor.* (DG)

Right: *Princetown Station, c.1900.* (DG)

Above: *A view of Princetown Station, 1955.* (DG)

Right: *A guard's van at Princetown Station.*

Above: *Prison officers and police search for an escaped convict, 1931.* (RJ)

Left: *Derek Roper and police Mini-Moke, 1967.* (DR)

Above: *Mrs Dawe directs Derek Roper, 1969.* (DR)

Left: *Bloodhounds being presented with an escaped convict's shoe to encourage the search, c.1930.* (RJ)

*Tyrwhitt Road runs north out of Princetown. The road entering the photograph
from the left is the path of the horse-drawn railway and old lines can just be
seen here as they cross the foreground and run to the right where they led to
the Railway Inn.*

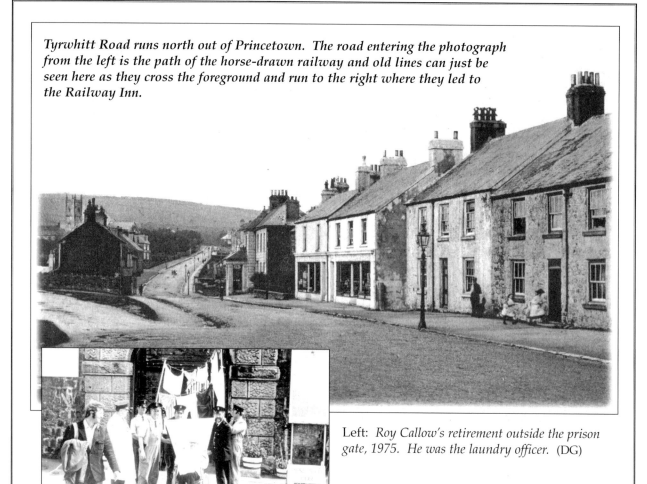

Left: *Roy Callow's retirement outside the prison
gate, 1975. He was the laundry officer.* (DG)

Below: *Princetown Carnival in Station Road,
looking south-east, late 1940s. Mr Wallace used
the van to deliver groceries.* (DC)

Left: *Princetown Carnival in Tavistock Road with New Villas (left), early 1950s.* (DC)

Gillie Warne as a baby.

Princetown Carnival, 1947. Diana (Carnival Queen), Gloria and Judith at the junction of Moor Crescent with Hessary Terrace. (FO)

Gillie Warne driving the prison tractor outside New Villas, at the carnival, August 1947. Mavis Sinclair is on the trailer (left) with Joyce Mead (right). Dave Moore is walking with his hands in his pockets. (AG)

Crowning the Carnival Queen (Sylvia Worth) at Princetown Carnival with Revd Reece, the prison chaplain (back left). (DC)

Left: *Two postmen beside the post van from Buckland Monachorum which went to Yelverton via Princetown.* (DG)

Below: *Policemen and ponies outside Devonshire House.* (RJ)

Below: *The Prince of Wales Hotel.* (DG)

David Pinkham in his toy car (right), *1945. His father was the landlord of The Prince of Wales.* (DG)

Mrs Pinkham outside The Prince of Wales pub, 1945. (DG)

Above: *Outside the Old Mortuary, December 1944. Left to right, back: Gladys Cooper and sister Doris Martin; front: Brian and David Cooper. (DC)*

Below: *Old Mortuary Steps, 2003.*

The school and the Prince of Wales pub, 2002.

The Prince of Wales Hotel offering bed and breakfast. (DG)

Above: *Hector Cribbett's lorry outside Devonshire House during Princetown Carnival.* (HC)

Left: *H.G. Cribbett, coal merchant.* (HC)

Above and right: *Princetown Town Hall was demolished in 1988. It stood next to The Prince of Wales pub. The site now provides Methodist homes for the elderly at Royal Court.* (DG)

Laying the foundation-stone of the Town Hall. Left to right: *Charlie Lean, Ted Owen, Robert Cruse, ?.* (FO)

Office (which may be relocated) and **Princetown Library**.

The Prince of Wales public house was opened in 1854 after the closure of the Rundlestone Inn.[7] Its brewery was the first run in conjunction with a public house in Princetown and Fred Jakeman was the publican during the Second World War. The road that cuts through the car park leads to the old railway. A fountain, provided by Mr Hooker in 1908, stands at the roadside and bears inscriptions:

T.R. Hooker, D.C.,
The gift of
R.H. Hooker Esq.

This fountain is erected
In grateful acknowledgment
Of the benefits received
From the life-giving air
Of Princetown

Princetown Town Hall was built around 1928 and was a fine building with two front entrances and two

A rear view of Princetown Co-op. (LC)

Above: *Co-operative Society foundation-stone.* (FO)
Below: *The Hooker fountain and the Town Hall.* (FO)

at the back. In the days before television its dance floor and stage served as the venue for concerts, dances, bands and a twice-weekly cinema. Whist drives, a badminton club and furniture shows from Plymouth were also held there. The Town Hall was a busy place during the Second World War when it provided Youth Club facilities. In 1940 Winnie Cooper held her wedding reception at the hall, as did many others. At this time Walter (Ted) and Olive Owen were caretakers and lived in the flat below the building and behind the Duchy Office.

Over the years hospitality has been extended to King George VI, Queen Elizabeth II and Prince Charles at the Town Hall and also at the Two Bridges Hotel. The Duchy handed the hall over to the council but its upkeep was deemed too expensive and it was demolished in 1988. The flooring was used in farm buildings in Rundlestone and the stage curtains, donated by Prince Charles, now adorn the stage at Postbridge Village Hall.

Attached to the south end of the Co-op was a one-storey wooden building belonging to the **W.H. Smith** chain of newsagents; Mr Desbrow ran the shop and lived at 9 Plymouth Hill. William Cribbett also worked here. W.H. Smith himself built a country mansion on the road to Moretonhampstead which later became the Manor House Hotel; he died within a year of its completion in 1913.

In May 1868 Mr Babb, who ran the Post Office, decided that the temporary accommodation offered

Left: *The Town Hall with the Co-op visible on the right.* (FO)

PRINCETOWN AMATEUR DRAMATIC SOCIETY

Programme

Two One-Act Plays

PRICE TWOPENCE

Left and right: *A programme for the production of two one-act plays,* The Legend of Raike's Cross, *a thriller by Stewart Ready, and,* By Popular Request, *a comedy by Matt Taylor. Both plays were performed in the Town Hall by Princetown Amateur Dramatic Society.* (DG)

'THE LEGEND OF RAIKES CROSS'
A Thriller by Stewart Ready

Scene
A Room in a House in Buckinghamshire

Cast

Widdison	Mr. L. Varley
Christine Wells	Mrs. N. Holley
Dr. Spenlow	Mr. L. Walker
Mrs. Danvers	Mrs. L. R. McDonald
Lydia Janes	Mrs. M. E. Allen
Harley Armitage	Mr. L. A. Wilson
John Everard	Mr. A. E. Holley

Produced by Mr. J. B. TAYLOR

Stage Manager: Mr. A. ALLEN

INTERLUDE

'BY POPULAR REQUEST'
A Comedy by Matt Taylor

Scene
The Living-Room of Julia and Harold's Home
in a Provincial Town

Cast

Julia Herbert	Mrs. E. Mather
Harold Herbert	Mr. A. E. Holley
Mrs. Lovejoy	Mrs. D. E. Davies
Eddie Downing	Mr. L. Varley
O'Grady	Mr. J. B. Taylor
Daisy Duncan	Mrs. M. E. Allen
Sally	Mrs. D. Durling
Martha	Miss P. R. Sanders
Mrs. Smith	Mrs. K. B. Wilson

Produced by Mr. L. A. WILSON

GOD SAVE THE KING

Below: *A Christmas concert in Princetown Town Hall, c.1950.* (BC)

Above: *Remembrance Day parade, 1970s.* (LC)

Above: *Prince Charles in Princetown.* (DG)

Right: *Prince Charles* (centre) *decorating George Cole* (right) *with the Imperial Service Medal for 43 years in the prison service, 1984. Prison Governor Colin Heald is on the left.* (GC)

Above: *Princetown Football Club end-of-season presentation gathering in Princetown Town Hall, c.1950.* (DG)

Right: *Princetown United Football Club photographed during the 1950–51 season.* (DG)

Left: In 1949 Princess Elizabeth visited Princetown. She is pictured with Les Mutton on her left and Col Bill Roberts, land steward, behind her. She is shaking hands with Francis Williams on whose right is Fred Owen. Mrs Francis Williams is on the far right. (FO)

This image and right: *Brownies, Guides and schoolchildren outside Princetown Town Hall, 1949.* (AG)

Above: *Princess Elizabeth photographed outside the Town Hall during her visit to Princetown, 1949.* (BC)

Left: *The Prince of Wales and Les Mutton (on his left) at Princetown Town Hall, c.1969.* (BC)

Above, and left and far left: *Four views of the Dartmoor National Park Information Office which was situated in the Town Hall at Princetown.* (DG)

Right: *Buses on Tavistock Road.* (RJ)

Below: *Tavistock Road, Princetown, the Co-op and W.H. Smith in the one-storey building on the far left.* (FO)

Above: *A bus outside Princetown Post Office, 1960. Left to right, back row: Bob Finch, ?, Mrs Finch, Granfa Cribbett, Ivy Worth, ?, Charlie Hinton, Bill Collins, Duncan Straughan, Sidney Hext, Sam Eva, Eggar Rook, Henza Cooper, Neggar (Nigel) Mead; front: Bill Gough, Thurza Cribbett, Mrs Stephens, Mrs Stephens, Mrs Hinton, Mrs Cooper, Clara Hext, Cecil Crocker, Mrs Lowry, Anne Hawkins, Polly Ball, ?, Mrs Rook, Mrs Mead, Mrs Tom French.*

Above: *Truscott's of Launceston ran charabanc tours in solid-tyred vehicles from which the passengers would have to dismount on steep hills. This photograph includes: Ivor Stephens, in the front of the charabanc; Clara wearing a black hat (back row, left of centre) and Lylie and Sidney (to the left of her); Gran Williams is in a black hat and coat (above the vehicle insignia) with Alice Stephens seated next to her (on right). Behind Gran is Aunt Hetta and behind her is Uncle Albert Meade. Mrs Youngson, wearing a hat, is seated in the back of the charabanc.* (BH)

The Ladies' Club carnival float. (DG)

Above: *The building which had housed the Youth Club, the Co-op and Bolt's Store was demolished in 1988. In this photograph the Youth Club stands to the right of The Prince of Wales, where Royal Court (inset, under construction (RJ))* is now situated. *(FO)*

Right: *The demolition of the Co-op.* (TS)

Below: *The Co-op, later the Youth Club, in Tavistock Road, Princetown.* (FO)

Right: *The Co-op before demolition with the steps of the Town Hall just visible (left).* (RJ)

Above: *Trial of the prison mutineers at Princetown Town Hall, 1932. Bolt's Store is on the right.* (DR)

Left: *Bolt family graves in Princetown churchyard, north of the church, 2003.*

Above: *A letter to the Duchy from Mr Babb who ran the Post Office and wished to erect a new building, 1868.*

Left: *The abattoir behind Bolt's Store.* (JW)

Royal Court. (FO)

there was inconvenient and he applied to erect a new Post Office on land near The Prince of Wales Inn.

Royal Court, a block of six flats, is a Methodist home for older people. This sheltered accommodation was built on the site of the Town Hall. The Co-op was constructed at the end of the nineteenth century and was purchased by Dingley Bolt in 1921 when it became Top Shop or **Top Bolts**, selling mainly hardware. Dingley Bolt ran the shop and kept the accounts for the extensive Bolt business in the town. He was also a local correspondent for the *Western Morning News* and reported on the 1932 prison mutiny, which was watched by many of the inhabitants of Princetown. The rioters were held at Dartmoor Prison and were sent, manacled, to the assizes at the Duchy Hotel each day until Friday 13 May when they were sentenced and transported to other prisons *(see photograph opposite, top)*.

On ascending the steps at Bolt's, a visitor would find the china department on the right-hand side and the main part of the store to the left. The shop stocked gas, paraffin and lamps, brushes, watches, records, and cameras and film. A visiting tradesman collected the films for development and returned them the following day.

The Masonic Lodge was at the top of the stairs and Peter Bolt, who was born there along with his

The foundations of Royal Court during construction. (RJ)

sister Margaret, recalls the sound of singing at the weekly meetings. Albert Wesley Bolt was a member of the Benevolence Lodge (No. 666) at Princetown. Behind Bolt's Top Shop was the **abattoir** that supplied the store. In 1950 Bolt's Top Shop became the Youth Club, established with capital of £1,000, although one room was used as the doctor's surgery. Subsequently the building was demolished and Royal Court was built on the site, opposite the entrance to the playing-fields.

The following memorials to the Bolt family can be found in Princetown churchyard:

> *In loving memory of*
> *Ewart*
> *Beloved husband of*
> *Lena Bolt,*
> *Who passed to rest*
> *August 4th 1954*
> *Aged 58 years*
>
> *Remembering*
> *Maude Louise Mary Bolt 1884–1966*
> *In heavenly love abiding*
>
> *In loving memory of Albert*
> *the dearly beloved husband of*
> *Mary Bolt,*
> *Who died Sep. 5th, 1958, Aged 46 years.*
> *"He giveth his beloved sleep."*
> *"Only good night beloved – not farewell."*
>
> *Also of Mary Amelia,*
> *His devoted wife*
> *Who was called home Nov. 16th 1939*
> *Aged 77 years.*
> *Loved by all.*

Between Royal Court and Venville House is **Duchy House**, a large guest-house and tearoom. The Finches ran **Venville House**, known as Top Finch's, and sold many items, predominantly food and some drapery. At the time of writing this is an old people's home. A memorial to John Finch in Princetown churchyard reads:

> *Sacred*
> *To [the] memory of*
> *John Finch*
> *Who departed this life*
> *June 19th 1867,*
> *Aged 47 years*
> *He was a kind and affectionate*
> *Husband, a loving Father, and*
> *Respected by all who knew him*

Station Road is another route to the site of Princetown Station. On the left or south side is a

Above: *Louis Brown* (left) *with Olive Brown and Maureen Ellis on a motorcycle outside 4 Station Road, 1958.* (LB)

Above: *4 Station Road, 1957. Left to right: Olive Brown, Shirley Ellis and Ivy Worth.* (LB)

The Cooper family with friends in Hessary View, looking towards North Hessary Tor with Woodville Avenue back left. Left to right: Brian Cooper, David Cooper, Alan Cooper (on bicycle crossbar), *Peter English, David English, Nigel Cooper, Rex Sinclair, Graham Sinclair.* (DC)

Above: *Olive Brown outside 4 Station Road, 1957.*
(LB)

Above: *Celia Cooper, Sam Cooper's widow, who lived to the age of 99, outside the cottages in Station Road.* (DC)

Right: *Olive Brown on her 90th birthday at 9 Moorland view.* (AS)

Alf Brown bathing Pearl, his Pomeranian dog, outside 4 Station Road, Princetown, 1947. The property was later demolished. (LB)

single dwelling followed by three semi-detached properties. The road swings to the right and passes the **Duchy Yard** and, after a left turn, leads into **Moorland View**, a row of five semi-detached houses on the north side built in 1927 on the site of **Babb's Clay Works**. Opposite Moor Gate and into Woodville Avenue is the site of a rifle range which was used following the Second World War and demolished in 2000. Finally the main road turns west again, passing a footpath to the churchyard and a path running up to North Hessary Tor. The two rows of houses here comprise **Hessary View** with two further semi-detached properties at **Moorland View.**

Back at Tavistock Road is the area where a pony patrol with rifles was posted to control traffic towards the prison. **Moor View Villas** and **Windsor Villas** are two pairs of semi-detached houses standing back a little from the road. **Keystones,** a private residence, used to be the Police House, with a police office on the north end replacing the old Police Station and its cells. Policing of the town provided for three distinct populations – the prison and its staff, the locals, and the tourists. Derek Roper policed the town from 1967 until 1972.

Kimberley Grange, the old vicarage, is a large house on the left-hand side. One of its past occupants, Revd Courtney Johns, is remembered for combining his love of riding with his work and visiting his parishioners on a large white horse. A small man, he wore a top hat and rode to hounds. He could not drive, however, and his wife, Thora, ferried

Top: *The inscription at Keystones.*

Above: *Kimberley Grange, 2003.*

Below: *Moorland View, 1927. Harry Halfyard is third from the left.* (DG)

The Halfyards when building Moorland View, 1926. Left to right, back row: Harry Halfyard, Neal Mead, Friendship ?, Alf Jutson, Jack Halfyard, Fred Pengelly; front: *Tom Geoffrey, Bill Halfyard, Reg Oxenham, Albert Mead.* (DG)

Above: *A horse and cart travelling north out of Princetown.* (RO)

Left: *Tavistock Road looking north.* (RJ)

The interior of Princetown Church before (above) *and during* (right) *restoration in 2003.* (JW)

Above: *A view from Princetown Church tower looking north over the prisoners' gravestones, 2003.*

Below: *Five views from Princetown Church tower, 2003.*

him around in a Rover 90 car. The couple retired to Kilmington in East Devon.

Princetown Parish Church[8] (not to be confused with the prison chapel) is dedicated – in common with many other churches at high altitudes, including Brentor – to St Michael and All Angels; it was thought that the Devil liked to land at high spots on the landscape and St Michael was regarded as a suitable deterrent. Princetown lies within the large Parish of Dartmoor Forest, which was created in 1989; before that date Lydford Parish included the whole area.

In 1810 the construction of the church was begun by French prisoners of war, who laboured in appalling conditions for sixpence a day. American prisoners fitted out the interior and the building was opened on 2 January 1814. The church was originally intended to have a peal of bells; however, they had only been transported as far as Plymouth when war was declared and they were hung instead in the Chapel of Devonport Dockyard. In 1868 the church was gutted by fire and was restored immediately. The large east window, a memorial to the American prisoners of war, was presented in 1910 by the National Society of United States Daughters of 1812.[9] The eighteenth-century pulpit came from St Sidwell's Church in Exeter. On the wall of the north aisle is a memorial to Thomas Tyrwhitt which declares that 'his name and memory are inseparable from the great works of Dartmoor.'

The exterior of the church has been altered by the addition of a porch at the north-west corner and aisle windows have been added to the original four on each side. Eden Phillpotts describes the building of the church in his novel *The American Prisoner* as:

Above: *A view from Princetown Church tower, 2003.*

Above right: *A view from Princetown Church tower looking east towards the prison, 2003.*

Right: *Repairs being made to Princetown Church, 2003. This photograph shows the north wall and the porch.*

Below: *Two signs on the gates of Princetown Church, 2003.*

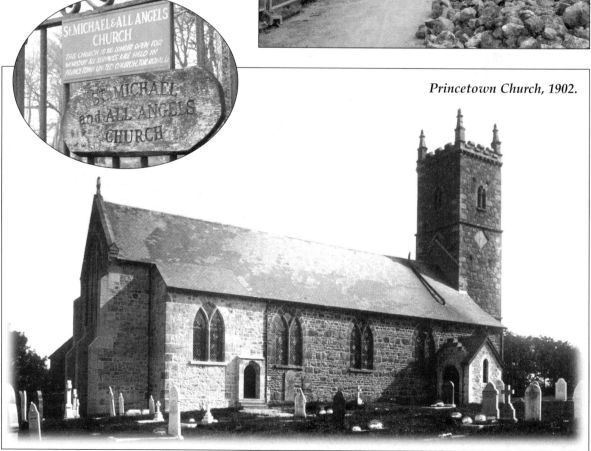

Princetown Church, 1902.

Above: *An old view of Princetown Church.* (JW)

Inset: *Cladding surrounds Princetown Church tower during renovation work, 2002.*

Left: *Ponies in the snow near Princetown Church, 1963.* (SA)

Right: *His Royal Highness the Prince of Wales (later King George V) leaving Princetown Church after the induction service of the new vicar, June 1919. The Lord Bishop of Exeter leads the procession, followed by Archdeacon A.W.T. Browne and local clergy. The Prince is just emerging from the doorway.* (DG)

Left: *The scene at the dedication of Princetown Parish Church with the Cub and Brownie Standards.* (DG)

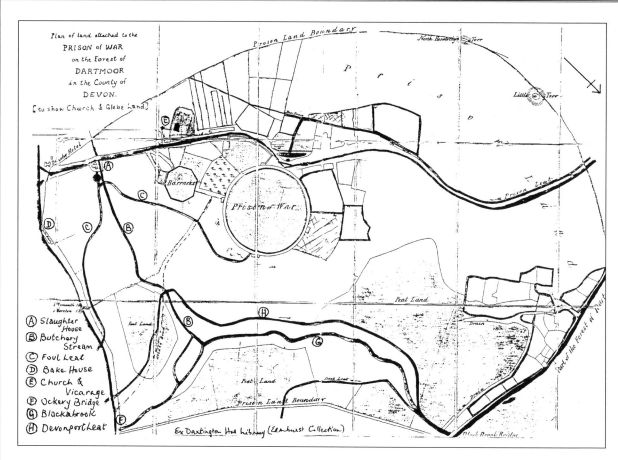

A plan of the land attached to the war prison in the Forest of Dartmoor, Devon, showing Church and glebe land. (DG)

Above: *Hoar frost coats the ornate gates of Princetown Church in February 1996.* (AG)

Right: *John Frederick Waycott, churchwarden and retired prison officer, 1909.* (JW)

Left: *Princetown Church covered in amil frost during the winter of 1995/6.* (TS)

Prisoners' gravestones in the churchyard, 2002.

... a rugged granite building, bare and sparsely decorated. One cannot observe the church, standing on such a high point of the moor, without imagining the terrible weather conditions endured by those working on its construction. On Dartmoor, as in Northumberland, amil frost or rime frost is caused by freezing fog, wind and temperatures below zero.[10]

Princetown churchyard includes monuments to many local people from the families of Bellamy, Cole, Conduit, Cooper, Cornish, Cribbett, Cruse, Halfyard, Hannaford, Langton, Mead, Perkins, Phillips, Rich, Rook, Rowe, Smith, Spurrell, Stephens, Wade, Waycott, Worth and Youngson. Peter Bolt's grandfather's grave is close to the church entrance and there are Bolts buried at the west end of the churchyard, near the hedge. Between 15 November 1815, when 27-year-old William Shillingford from the Barracks was the first to be buried, and 23 September 2002, some 1,204 bodies have been interred. Small granite stones bearing initials and a date of death mark prisoners' graves in several rows. Another stone, that of a Borstal boy, is closer to the church.

The **Chaplain's House** was built around 1850 for the prison chaplain and is now a private dwelling. It is said to be the most haunted house in the town.

Ron Joy, a prison officer, and two convicts built the **bus shelter**.

Woodville Avenue extends to the west. Church Row (built nearby c.1809–1815) was renamed Chapel Row, then Government Row and finally Woodville Terrace. The terrace of eight houses, in one of which Dissenters at one time held services, was demolished during the 1960s.

Woodville Cottages were destroyed and replaced by an extended circuit of Cornish units, which were themselves demolished in 2002. Two new four-bedroomed detached houses may be erected on this site. Cornish units were rapidly erected properties, that did not call for the slow process of bricklaying and were used to provide accommodation for prison staff. In the early 1980s a housing allowance was negotiated for prison staff instead of housing provision and this gave them the freedom to purchase property outside the town. Shop trade in the town deteriorated and the Cornish units stood empty for years before being allocated to families from beyond the area. The lower parts of some have been rebuilt in brick, and Rayburns and Baxi fires installed.

The movement of prison staff to accommodation outside Princetown, the closure of the railway and the installation of cattle grids to keep ponies out of the town all heralded decline for this once busy area. Today, although some villages around Dartmoor are saturated in terms of population, Princetown is not so crowded, perhaps due to the proximity of the prison and the harsh weather conditions. A Napoleonic prisoner at Dartmoor during the early 1800s described the locality as 'truly Siberian'.

Next to Woodville Cottages, to the north, was the **farm manager's house** incorporating the Catholic church in front. At the time of writing the nearest Catholic church is at Yelverton.

The **water tower** was used to store water for the prison. The water reached the tower from the **prison leat** which channels water south from the River Walkham for some four miles; the overflow goes to the West Dart River.

The **prison farm** appears next on the left. Two shepherds looked after a large flock of sheep and a herd of Galloway cattle, whilst some 32 prisoners

Prisoners' gravestones and Princetown Church, 2002.

The southern gateway into the churchyard. The prisoners' graves are visible, 2003.

Left: *A memorial to 'Three Valiant Soldiers' on the south wall of the churchyard. Joseph Penton, Patrick Carlin and George Driver of the 7th Royal Fusiliers died on the way up from Dousland for duty in February 1853.*

Left: *A lone 1946 monument to a prisoner in Princetown churchyard*

Above: *Two early gravestones in Princetown churchyard, south of the church, 2003.*

Above: *The old Chaplain's House, Princetown, 2002.*

Right: *Woodville Avenue in the late 1970s.* (RJ)

Dartmoor Prison from the air. (FO)

Above: *Woodville Avenue, 1963.*

Left: *Two brothers, Jack (left) and Gordon Worth, in Woodville Avenue in the snow of 1947. Jack, the blacksmith, shod horses at his shop behind The Railway Inn and Gordon was explosives expert at Merrivale Quarry and then at the prison quarry.* (GC)

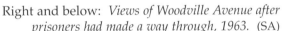

Right and below: *Views of Woodville Avenue after prisoners had made a way through, 1963.* (SA)

Cliff Waycott cleaning the Devonport Leat. **(FO)**

Below: *Prison farm buildings, used as the Prison Museum in 2002.*

Above: *The old water tower outside the entrance to Dartmoor Prison, 2002.*

Below: *An aerial view of Dartmoor Prison showing the circular wall.* (FO)

worked on the farm and tended the gardens and the sports field, undertook the indoor work and helped with the animals, some of this work being undertaken with the help of the 12 Shires on the farm. A pond was built in the grounds for swimming. The pony patrol, which carried guns that frightened the horses, walked the fields with two dogs. George Cole joined in 1941 as the prison shepherd, later using a pony and then a very large horse for his work. He spent 43 years in the prison service and the prisoners worked with him. Sheep shearing was carried out initially by hand and later the first mechanical shears were introduced. George's boss was Mr Cecil Frampton, the prison farm manager, formerly a prison officer.

The **Prison Museum** now stands on the site of the old milking parlour where the traffic used to be stopped to allow the cattle to be taken across the road for milking. Grass was dried and converted to grass nuts which were stored above the dairy. On one occasion this flammable stockpile caught fire, creating a blaze that led to the closure of the road for an entire week.

Mandy Bacon (née Owen), Fred Owen's daughter, exercised Zorro each day during the 1978 blizzard.

Princetown has seen very severe winters over the centuries. The great blizzard of 1891 was notoriously fierce[11 & 12] and the year 1941 saw incredibly tough blizzards as well; Dr Lindsay from Tavistock visited Princetown three times on one fearful day for obstetric reasons. The winter of 1943 saw cattle freeze in groups, surrounded by ice, and a number of ponies froze to death where they stood. The winter of 1947 was the coldest the town had seen; cattle once again froze to death, telegraph lines came down and tractors froze on their way back to the farms. There was more snow in 1963 but it was not as cold.[13 & 14] The prison delivered bread to the village in the bucket of a bulldozer, which was much appreciated.

The *Western Morning News* reported on the weather:

8 January – A sheep on Dartmoor was attacked by a fox and eaten alive.

9 January – More food was dropped to the starving sheep, cattle and ponies on the Moor and there was a heavy loss among sheep and cattle. These were fed from helicopters from Chivenor and 5 tons of hay was dropped on the northern fringe of Dartmoor in the preceding 48 hours.

10 January – Commandos, Civil Defence workers and RSPCA officials based a search around Great Mis Tor and a 100 men were involved rescuing the animals.

11 January – Roads were closed and snowdrifts on the Okehampton line marooned three rail engines.

15 January – Helicopters operated from the Yelverton area to locate ponies and sheep in the more remote parts of Dartmoor.

19 January – Four missing Plymouth stationed soldiers sheltered in old Dartmoor tin miners' cottage at Whiteworks, 2 miles south east of Princetown and 3 miles from Devil's Elbow where they had been dropped by lorry 3 days previously for a 24-hour training exercise over about 10 miles of wild moorland. Food and Calor gas in the cottage together with their rations enabled them to survive.

31 January – Six inches of snow covered Dartmoor the preceding evening. By mid-afternoon the Tavistock to Princetown Road was blocked by deep drifts between Foggintor School and Rundlestone Cross and traffic was unable to get through even with chains. The drifts prevented two Plymouth magistrates and the Home Office magistrate from London, who were members of the Panel of Justices visiting the prison, from getting home and they were put up for the night. The prison lorry could not get through to Tavistock and prisoners going from Tavistock to Princetown were held up too.

4 February – Heavy fall of snow started at 5am. Princetown policeman Constable Colin Evans said over the telephone that heavy snow was falling 'but it is coming straight down and there is very little wind.'

Helicopter took 56lbs of yeast, 12 dozen tins of evaporated milk and two cases of dried milk from Kelly College to the prison where the bakery supplied the town. A group of villagers battled their way through thick drifts from Princetown to Merrivale where a bread delivery van had been stuck fast in the snow and loaded 300 loaves into sacks and trudged back to the village.

9 February – A photograph on the preceding day showed some snow was disappearing.

Tor View is a terrace of six houses provided for prison farm workers. The gasman lived at No. 2. In 1941 George Cole moved here from Red Cottages instead of moving into prison accommodation at Devonshire House.

From here the road to Rundlestone is bounded by low stone walls punctuated by many blocked gateways. The prison leat runs high above on the hillside to the west but as the road climbs it

Left: *Prison quarry.* (RJ)

Below: *The prison quarry with a derelict watch-tower.* (RJ)

Right and below: *A helicopter dropping yeast and other products on the prison sports field, 1963.* (SA)

The road to Rundlestone, 1963. (SA)

The entrance to the prison quarry, 2002.

eventually becomes level with the waterway. Scant remnants of the birch trees may be seen, many of which were cut down to prevent their branches, heavy with snow and ice, from falling on passing vehicles.

Some 30 prisoners worked in the **prison quarry** under the watchful eye of an armed guard situated in the tower near the entrance. Stone from the quarry was used for the Devonport Leat and during the Second World War Nissen huts were erected on the site. The quarry closed around 1975.

At the point where the road joins the Two Bridges to Tavistock road is **Rundlestone Corner**. Here, on the west side, was Rundlestone Corner Pond, later filled in, into which all sorts of junk was cast including prams and shell cases from the war. The name is sometimes given as Rendlestone.

The **Rundle Stone** itself marked the boundary of the prison land and stood on the north of the road just west of a milestone and opposite another stone on the south side of the highway, probably in line with the east boundary of the road to North Hessary Tor transmitter. Crossing[15] stated that the name Rundlestone is taken from a granite pillar or long stone that stood on the boundary of Dartmoor Forest. The letter R was cut into the top. Crossing wrote:

It is not named as a bondmark in surveys, but was, however, recognised as such in 1702. It was formerly to be seen on the south of the way, immediately opposite

to the modern boundary stone, which we shall observe on the left. This bears the names of the parishes that here meet each other – Lydford and Walkhampton – and on passing it we again enter the Forest. The Rundle Stone was broken up several years ago, when a wall was built nearby. It is much to be regretted that an ancient landmark should have been wantonly destroyed; unfortunately the spoliator has been busy in Dartmoor, and has swept away many interesting objects. About the year 1881 I took measurements of the Rundle Stone. It stood 7 feet about the stones at which it was set, and was 4 feet in girth. It is marked on a map dated 1720 as 'great stone call'd roundel'.

Hansford Worth, a great explorer of Dartmoor, also wrote of the Rundle Stone:

Admittedly this post did not lie on the bounds of the Forest, as set forth in the earlier Perambulations, or as now recognised: which is a straight joining North Hessary Tor and Mis Tor pan. And, further, it offered no feature corresponding to its name. But, if we abandon this identification, and give to 'rundle' the meaning of 'roundel', we have, in Rundlestone Tor, a natural object which fulfils all the conditions; it lies on the precise line of the boundary, and presents good reason for its name; a 'roundel', in common parlance, as in heraldry, was a small circular object. The principal feature of Rundlestone Tor, which I take to be the

Rundlestone Road, 28 February 1916. (RO)

Through the woods to Rundlestone, 1963. (SA)

The road to Rundlestone Corner before deforestation (above, (FO)) and after the destruction of the birch trees (below).

Above: *The road to Rundlestone in the snow of 1963.* (DC)

Left: *Hector Cribbett at Rundlestone Corner, February 1947.* (HC)

Right: *The milestone at Rundlestone Corner, 2003.*

Below: *George Cole with sheep at Rundlestone Corner, looking east. Pascoe's Cottage is visible in the background.* (GC)

The road to Rundlestone looking south, 1940s, and Alf Brown (inset) at Rundlestone Big House, 1942. (LB)

original Rundlestone, is a great sloping mass of granite; it has in it one rock basin, 28in. in diameter, and, on the average, perhaps 7in. in depth. The Rundlestone now measures 23 feet by 23 feet.

Mining interests on Dartmoor were largely in the hands of John Gill and John Rundle who suggested that a direct road link be built from Tavistock, over Dartmoor, to Exeter. The Rundle Stone might have represented the site of a toll-house or other starting point for the journey over the moor.

The return from Rundlestone to Princetown (see

The gateposts of Rundlestone Big House (left, in the wall) and the curve in the wall at the site of the old cattle grid close to Rundlestone Corner looking south on Tavistock Road.

Rundlestone Big House and Rundlestone Pond. (DY)

page 87) down the east side of the road gives fine views over the eastern moor, to Beardown Tors and others on the horizon and, more distant, Hameldon, Haytor, Saddle Tor and Rippon Tor.

The **Rundlestone Inn**, built during the 1830s when the name Paul Rendle first appears, was situated at Rundlestone Corner. New House (later called the Warren House Inn) and possibly the Dartmoor Inn at Merrivale are shown on Donn's map of 1765, and in 1772 Judge Buller erected the Saracen's Head at Two Bridges.[16]

The landlord was Hugh Hill and his daughter, Mary Ann, married Richard Crowle from St Austell in 1831. She and her husband were among many selected from Cornwall for assisted emigration. They embarked on the *Harry Lorrequer*[17] at Plymouth on 21 September 1849 and arrived at Port Adelaide on Boxing Day of 1849. The family spent two years in South Australia before moving to Victoria during the early gold rush period in 1852. They prospered there and today their descendants live in Australia.

During the period 1851–62 William Friend was tenant of the Rundlestone Inn, another mid-nineteenth-century landlord being Mr Hannaford. In 1861 there were two men named Hugh Hill living at Blackabrook; Hugh Hill of the inn was 74 and a farmer (who was listed as being back at Rundlestone by 1871, although still farming), and the other Hugh Hill was 53 and a stoker at Princetown's gasworks.

It seems that the Rundlestone Inn must have closed not long after this as it was not open for business at the time of its sale in February 1882, when it was sold with more than 26 acres of land which included Church Park dwelling house and two fields called Ruck Park and West of the Leat. The inn was taken over by the prison in order to provide prison accommodation in two semi-detached houses known as **Rundlestone Big House.** This is thought to have been the same building as it boasted six large iron

Left: *A 'No Stopping' sign on the road from Rundlestone Corner, the prison is in the background (left), 2002.*

Right: *Cecil Frampton (centre) with two officers in the prison farmyard, east of the road to Rundlestone.* (RF)

A prize herd of sheep with Tor View in the middle. (RF)

Above: *Prison farm fields, looking east, 2002.*

Below: *Prison stable block, 2002.*

Left: *George Cole exhibiting a prize sheep from the prison farm at Exeter sheep shearing, c.1950.* (GC)

Below: *Five prize rams at the prison before sale and transfer to Scotland.* (RF)

Six crossbreed cattle with George Cole (far right) at the prison farm, c.1980. (GC)

Ron Cribbett with a wagon used to transport grass cuttings. Cecil Frampton, prison farm manager, accomplished his ambition of growing high-quality grass on the moor for the production of grass nuts. (RF)

hooks suspended from the ceiling which probably supported hams to feed visitors at the former pub.

Fine gardens surrounded the property and water for washing came from the prison leat through a pipe, which passed under the road and the house, into a shute. Drinking water came from a tap at Rook's House, Rundlestone, until mains water from the pumping house arrived in 1938.

The gateposts of both the large and small gates are still visible but the round area, where the dray may have dropped barrels for the inn after backing in through the large gate, has disappeared. The wall curves sharply inwards where a gate was once situated enabling horses and others to bypass the cattle grid.

The northernmost and larger part of Rundlestone Big House faced north and was home to Eric Green from 1945 until 1952. The property was demolished in 1957. The southern part faced the road and the entrance was down a step. Here a copper, fuelled by wood from the plantation, was situated for washing the clothes and a right turn into the kitchen (on the west side of the building) revealed the black cooking range with its two-gallon water tank at the side. There was a pantry or cold-room and fresh water was obtained from a cow-handle pump at the water-works at Rundlestone Corner. The earth closet was outside and was emptied twice each week by prisoners with a horse and cart conveying a half-barrel to transport the effluent. Donald Warne was born in the house in 1930 and lived there until 1947, after which

it was occupied by George, a stone worker, and May Easterbrook. The property was subsequently demolished and stone from the building used to elevate the car parking area behind Great Mis Lodge.

Dartmoor Prison, about which several histories have been published,[17a–26] then comes into view beyond a conifer plantation. The prison is surrounded by one mile of walling, most of it in circular form. The entrance bears the inscription *Parcere Subjectis*, from Virgil (70–19BC):

Excudent alii spirantia mollius aera (Credo equidem),
Vivos ducent de marmore vultus,
Orabunt causus melius, caelique meatus
Describent radio et surgentia sidera dicent:
Tu regere imperio populos, Romane, memento
(Hae tibi erunt artes) pacique imponere morem,
PACERE SUBJECTIS ET DEBELLARE SUPERBOS.

This translates as:

Others shall shape bronzes more smoothly so that they
*   seem alive (yes, I believe it),*
Shall mould from marble living faces,
Shall better plead their cases in court,
And shall demonstrate with a pointer the motions of the
*   heavenly bodies and tell the stars as they rise:*
You, Roman, make your task to rule nations by your
*   government*
(These shall be our skills), to impose ordered ways upon
*   a state of peace*
TO SPARE THE VANQUISHED AND TO SUBDUE
*   THE ARROGANT.*

Boundary stones indicate the extent of the prison land, both rough-cut and small flat-faced stones, bearing an arrow and the letters 'DCP' indicating 'Directors of Convict Prisons' (not Dartmoor County Prison). These are most easily seen in Mistor Lane.

Police notices indicate 'NO STOPPING' in this area. Although essentially intended to prevent communication with prisoners, the notices may also help to make this dangerous road a little safer.

On the north side of the entrance to the prison is the old Deputy Governor's House. On the south side

(continues page 74)

Princetown seen from North Hessary Tor. (FO)

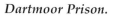

PRISON COMMISSION,

HOME OFFICE, WHITEHALL, S. W.

5 April 1900.

In reference to your application, dated 1st February 1900 you are informed that you have been appointed Assistant Warder in the Prison Service, on probation, and you are requested to report yourself to the Governor of Wormwood Scrubs Prison, for duty as soon as possible.

You are required to join the Prison at your own expense, and to undergo an examination by a Medical Officer of the Establishment Should you not then be considered medically fit for the Service, your appointment may be cancelled.

Your commencing rate of salary will be £ 60 per annum, with other emoluments, as under :—

(a) Uniform.
(b) Quarters, rent free, or, subject to certain conditions, an allowance of £9. 2s. per annum in lieu.
(c) Medical attendance (by the Medical Officer or his approved substitute only) and medicines for yourself, and, in certain circumstances, for your family also.

There are no other allowances of any kind, nor will you be permitted to receive any gratuity or perquisite whatever.

The salary and allowances of your office will not begin until you have actually commenced your duties ; nor will you be entitled to uniform until the confirmation of your appointment after the period of probation.

You will be liable to deductions from your salary, by way of fine, for neglect of duty or misconduct.

You will continue on probation until your appointment is confirmed or your engagement terminated. Your engagement will be terminated if, from observation of your general abilities and attention to duty, you are not considered likely to become a satisfactory Prison Officer ; or if, for medical reasons, you are not considered fit for the office to which you have been appointed on probation.

You will not be permitted to take any other occupation or employment, or to hold without special permission any other public office; and it will be part of your engagement to give such instruction or assistance in any trade with which you may be acquainted, as may be directed.

You will be required to act in strict conformity with the existing Orders and Regulations, and with such as may from time to time be established.

On joining the Prison you will be required, if married, to produce your Certificate of Marriage.

To Mr Edward Worth

for Secretary.

Left: *A prison commission for Edward Worth dated 5 April 1900. The commencing salary was £60 per annum with additional uniform, accommodation and medical attendance.* (DG)

Above: *Prison officers outside Dartmoor Prison.*

Dartmoor Prison.

Left: *Some small visitors for the prison officer, Edwin Jones, on horseback.* (DG)

Right: *Dartmoor Prison, 1945.* (HC)

Right: *Dartmoor Prison officers playing cricket in a field where the officers' football pitch is now situated. The cottages on the skyline, known as New London, are today hidden by trees.* (DG)

Above left: An aerial view of Princetown showing the prison surrounded by its perimeter wall, 1930. (DG)

Above right: Mr J. Waycott (left) was born in 1856 and died in 1936. He joined the prison service in 1885 and retired in 1907 but returned to the service for temporary duties at the outbreak of the First World War. He was described as 'one of nature's truest gentlemen' and 'friend and helper of all, enemy of none, a gracious and faithful character.' (DG)

Below: Prisoners pulling a cart out of the prison gateway. (JW)

Above: Dartmoor Prison. On the right is the old C block and on the left are the Blackabrook Flats, 30 in all. (HC)

Above: A Christmas card from a conscientious objector held in the prison, dated 1917. (FO)

Left: Dartmoor Prison and the moor beyond.

Prison Officers' Club, 2002.

Above: *Signs on the wall of Dartmoor Prison, 2002.*

Above: *Snow outside the prison gates, 1963.* (RF)

Below: *The prison gate.* (RJ)

Above: *An aerial view of Dartmoor Prison in the 1950s. The entrance to the prison is on the right-hand side of the picture. The road from Rundlestone to the Square goes past the water tower. In the prison, old C Hall is being demolished.* (RJ)

Dartmoor Prison from the Devonport Leat. (RJ)

Dartmoor Prison gate. (FO)

Left: *A group outside the prison. Left to right: Tom Metters, H. Cooper, ?, Ron Cribbett, Sonny Williams, Cecil Frampton, Mr Bennett (administrator at the prison).* (RF)

Below: *A view of Princetown showing Devonshire House.* (WS)

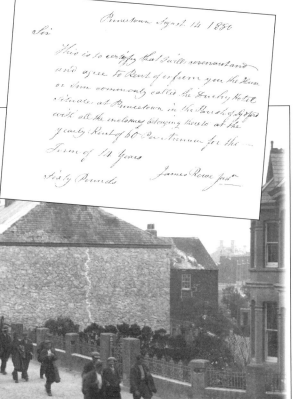

Above: *Dartmoor Prison with Great Mis Tor in the distance.* (FO)

Right: *Certificate of James Rowe regarding the rent of the Duchy Hotel, 14 August 1850, Princetown.* (DG)

Conscientious objectors returning from the prison. **(FO)**

This image: *Devonshire House in Tavistock Road.* **(LS)**

Below: *A memorial to Dr Buikeley Jones in Princetown churchyard.*

of the entrance is the old Governor's House, converted in 1991 after demolition of the Victorian extension and then rebuilt to provide a refreshments room for prison officers. Nowadays governors live away from the area. During the 1930s and '40s Major Charles Pannall was Governor, followed by Major Harvey; their uniform included heavy tweed plus-fours. Prisoners of war (1809–15) were allowed to live out on parole if they gave their word that they would not try to escape and they were billeted at Ashburton, Tavistock, Moretonhampstead and Okehampton, as well as at Crediton, North Tawton, South Molton and Tiverton. The in-house prisoners were allowed to travel up to a mile from the prison, and milestones or parole stones may still be seen on the boundaries.

Conscientious objectors were held at the prison during the First World War[27] and were employed in the prison work centre.[28] In 2001 the site was downgraded to a Category C prison for lower-risk inmates.

Numbers 1, 2 and 3 **New Villas** comprise a row of houses where senior officers used to live. St Michael's House, No. 3, is the vicarage. **Isca** was the Chief Officer's house which was later let.

The **Doctor's House**, set back from the road down a short drive, was known as AMOS (a medical officer's house) as each prison medical officer had to live here. John Mackintosh lived in Doctor's Cottage.

In an article published in the 1990s, Peter Trafford, a Senior Medical Officer in Her Majesty's Prison Medical Service, described the conditions in which the American prisoners of war lived during the years 1813–15.[29] At that time the outer stone wall of the prison was a mile long and 14 feet high. Plentiful fresh water was available from the prison leat which filled the reservoir outside the main gate and underground conduits then led to each of the principal buildings. Medical staff consisted of a surgeon, assistant surgeon, the matron and a seamstress, and supplies came by sea from Apothecaries' Hall in London (although leeches could be purchased locally!). Dr George McGrath was the principal and his assistant was Mr McFarlane.

A stone plaque on the southern wall of the churchyard reads:

Sacred to the Memory of
William Hutchinson Buikeley Jones M.D.
Staff Surgeon on Royal Navy
And late Medical officer of Dartmoor Prison
Died 11 April 1860 aged 61 years
Esteemed and beloved by a large circle of friends

Henry Rounce lived in the Doctor's House in 1861 and Herbert Smalloy lived at Doctor's Quarters in Princetown in 1881. From 1935 to 1944 Dr Roper was the prison medic.

Hisworthy, the former home of the Assistant Governor, stands on the corner of the widened

The 1852 inscription on the wall that once fronted Devonshire House.

Burrator Avenue. The building subsequently became the home of the prison farm manager. Burrator Avenue was known as Piano Street, due to the fact that almost every window seemed to contain an instrument. Just past this point stands a long wall with gateposts; the gateways have been filled in. A stone in the wall is marked with the date 1852. This is the site of **Devonshire House**, a massive building of three-storey flats that housed prison staff. Access was tedious and by way of a series of staircases without lengthwise corridors. Few staff wanted to live here but often were forced to do so until alternative accommodation could be found. The flats were demolished in 1968 and much of the stone deposited alongside the Devonport Leat near Roundhill Farm.

The regime was tough for those who moved into the area. Women usually arrived to marry prison officers, many of whom were ex-servicemen, and the divorce rate was amongst the highest in the country during the mid-twentieth century.

The Devonshire House flats, each with an old-fashioned grate and its blue-black walls invariably covered with grime, provided first married quarters. In 1936, when one 22-year-old London girl was accommodated in an apartment for her first year in Princetown, slates were missing from the roof and water ruined her mother's gift of new curtains and pooled on the floor. The work of

cleaning and decorating the flats fell to the prisoners, who also cleaned the streets and collected refuse. The men seem to have been friendly and willing to engage in conversation.

In the early-twentieth century prison officers' accommodation was provided in eight blocks, namely Blackabrook Flats (A block), Burrator Avenue (B, C and D blocks), Devonshire House (E block), Heather Terrace behind the Officers' Club (F block), Hessary Terrace (G block) and Moor Crescent (H block).

Blackabrook Flats stood behind Devonshire House. The two blocks were similar except that the 30 flats at Blackabrook had three bedrooms and Devonshire House units had only two. The flats in both buildings had one living-room. Long corridors ran the length of Blackabrook, forming an ideal area for children to play. During the Second World War the flats became the main victualling store and offices, and some 100 Nissen huts were situated where Blackabrook Avenue is now. Prison cells were used to store blankets and clothes, whilst tins and cartons were stored in the huts. Deliveries were made by 3-ton lorries, and later 6-tonners. A nearby brick shed housed a fire pump, rather like a transit van, during the war, but the shed was demolished in 2003.

At the south end of Devonshire House, where Barrack Road turns the corner and runs eastwards, a stone in the wall is dated 1853. The **Prison Officers' Club** or Recreation Rooms, now a listed building, provided cinema seats for sixpence a throw. A new club was built on at an angle but the listed building is now obsolete and boarded up. Further down Barrack Road is a gate lodge which would have been used by the prison when the back entrance, the traders' gate, was still in service. The lodge is now inhabited and is known as **Dart Cottage**.

Hessary Terrace, a long terrace of houses, appears next on Tavistock Road. At the end of the terrace **Moor Crescent** stretches to the east towards **Heather Terrace** and each of these roads provides good views of the moor.

Princetown School, opposite the old Town Hall, is constructed of stone and part-rendered. This

Michael Grigg outside Devonshire House, 1968. The buildings were demolished soon afterwards. (AG)

Last remnants of Devonshire House (left) after demolition in the 1960s. (RJ)

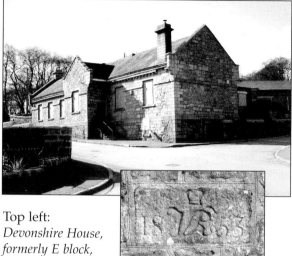

Top left: *Devonshire House, formerly E block, faces the church. These tall stone buildings had provision for a light above the doorways.* (DG)

Top: *The disused Prison Officers' Club.*

Above: *The 1853 inscription on the Prison Officers' Club.*

Above: *Looking up Burrator Avenue before road widening in the late 1980s.* (RJ)

Right: *Moor Crescent.*

Above: *Burrator Avenue (the left turn off Tavistock Road) before widening in the 1980s.* (RJ)

Right: *Gran Williams outside Heather Terrace, delivering milk. Formerly E block, this terrace was built in 1905.* (BH)

fee-paying school was provided for the children of those who worked at the prison and there were 40 or 50 children in each class. The headmaster's house was attached at the southern end of the school and from 1935 until 1944 headmasters in succession included Mr Burton, Mr Conduit and Mr Harrison.

The majority of children of families in Princetown attended the school until the age of 15, but some obtained a scholarship to attend the Grammar School in Tavistock. In 1961 Princetown became a primary school and at the age of 11 children went to Tavistock. Prison officers were once stationed at Princetown for seven years and more recently this has decreased to five. They now tend to live away from the town and many people are relative newcomers. Winnie Cooper worked at the school as a general kitchen assistant after she left Bolt's Store. 'Cheel' Williams (née Cooper) was the cook and prepared more than 200 dinners daily; at the time of writing there are barely 50 attendees.

Bellever Close provides a substantial amount of accommodation in a circuit of Cornish units.

The Temperance Movement was strong in England during the mid-nineteenth century and the **Imperial Hotel** was a Temperance House – a meeting-place for those who did not consume alcohol. The original Temperance Hotel was situated on Two Bridges Road. The Imperial Hotel was used during the First World War as a site in which sphagnum moss, collected from the moor, was treated and dried. This was used as a dressing for wounds. Some moss was collected during the Second World War but not to the same extent.[30] Later the hotel became the Post Office, a yellow building with accommodation above where mail was sorted. Bert Rose ran the Post Office until his son Jack took over. The doctor's surgery was based here at one time and Eric Cruse was born here. The

John Coulson's Good Scholar's Report from Princetown School, 28 July 1943. (DG)

building was demolished but the two K6 **red telephone kiosks** that stood in front are still in place (and functional).[31]

Helena Villa is an impressive home that once boasted bay windows. The monkey-puzzle tree outside grows well.

The next row of buildings was known as Frenchman's Row and encompassed a butcher's shop, a paper shop and general store, and the **Dartmoor Gift Shop**.[32] The Gift Shop was on the site of Bottom Finch's which sold mainly food and was run by the one-armed postman, Robert Finch.

The old **Methodist Chapel** behind the Gift Shop was used during the First World War for the preparation of iodine obtained from weeds collected on the moor. The demolition of a property in front of the chapel at the time of writing will allow access through to the building where living accommodation will be provided after conversion.

Herbert R. Lord (1872–1961), a stonemason, developed **Lord's Café** during the late 1930s following his return from America with his fortune.[33] Memorials to the Lord family may be seen in Princetown churchyard:

*IHS
in loving memory of
Jane
the beloved wife of GEORGE Lord
died August 23rd 1881 aged 67 years
'DEAR CHILDREN ARISE UP AND CALL HER
BLESSED:
HER HUSBAND ALSO. AND HE PRAISETH HER.'*

*Also of the above
George Lord,
Died December 1st 1899, aged 89 years.
'AT REST.'*

The playground north of Princetown School, 2002.

Princetown School, 2002.

Left: *Princetown School group, 1920s.* (JW)

Below: *Princetown School group, c.1900.* (RJ)

Below centre: *School sports.*

Above: *Princetown School group, 1940s.*

Above: *Princetown School.* Left to right, back row: *Henry Cooper, Paula Lidstone, Marcia Baker, Anne Ellicott, Edna Green, Ernie Metters;* third row: *Don Youngson, Gloria Halfyard, Joyce Green, Barbara Mead, Evelyn Sinclair, Gwenny Wilcox, Barbara Moore, Diane Majerison, Fred Owen, Mr Conduit;* second row: *Desmond Rooke, Gerald Worth, John Moore, George Moss, Eric Hext, Dereck Sinclair;* front: *Gordon Ward, ? Fitzgibbons, Mervyn Rich, Roger Cowie, Norman Cribbett.* (LC)

Above: *School singers, 1940s.*

Left: *Princetown School. Left to right, back row: Janet Baker, ?, Janet Gilpin, Esther Perkins, Beryl Davies, Jill Smith, Mrs Conduit, Mr Conduit (headmaster); third row: Kenneth Hext, ?, Elizabeth Rapson, Eve Ellicott, ?, ?, ?, Margaret Cole; second row: Derek Eden, Doreen Sinclair, ?, ?, Ann Warne, Ann Blackmore, Barbara Blackmore, Rosemary Stephens, Brian Cooper, Stewart Jasper; front: ?, ?, Michael Frampton, Keith Jones, Paul Stanger, ?, ?, ?, ?.* (AG)

Right: *Sports Day at Princetown School, 1952. Blackabrook Avenue has not yet been built behind the prison officers' playing-field.* (BC)

Above: *Princetown School class, 1947.* (FO)

Right: *The sack race at Princetown School Sports Day. The properties in Blackabrook Avenue are under construction.* (DC)

Above and right: *Infants at Princetown School.* (FO)

Left: *Princetown Home Guard outside the school, early 1940s.* (LC)

Below: *Laundry class in domestic science at Princetown School. Left to right: Beryl Davies, Elizabeth Rapson, Esther Perkins, Mrs Brown, Jill Smith, Barbara Blackmore, Mr Partridge (headmaster), Doreen Sinclair, Ann Warne. Sylvia Varney is in front.* (AG)

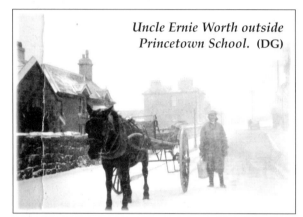

Uncle Ernie Worth outside Princetown School. (DG)

Left: *The Princetown postman, Bob Finch, in the post van (registration AYP 318) and Henry Moore* (right) *who used to sort the mail in the Imperial Hotel Post Office. The Royal Mail van was used to deliver the post to Princetown from Yelverton.* (DG)

Right: *Princetown School van outside the school, 1935.* (BH)

Above: *The Imperial Hotel, later Princetown Post Office, before its demolition.* (DG)

Inset: *Looking north out of Princetown with the Post Office on the right.* (RO)

Right: *The Post Office, formerly the Imperial Hotel.* (DG)

Princetown Post Office. (FO)

Right: *The old Post Office, 1912. Note the wooden scaffolding held together with rope.* (DG)

Lord's Café before development and, beyond, the Imperial Hotel advertising lunches and teas. Note the gas streetlights and early motor vehicles. The church can just be seen beyond the buildings on the left. (DG)

Lord's Cafe (right) and Helena Villa (left). (FO)

The Dartmoor Café in Princetown advertising junkets and cream, luncheons and teas, at the premises of H.R. Lord. The canopy over the building behind the streetlight advertises the Dartmoor Café. (DG)

Above: *The rear of Lord's Café and the old Methodist Chapel, east of Tavistock Road, 2003.*

Right: *The café to the right in Duchy Square advertises tea and coffee. Lord's Café is still situated to the north.* (DG)

Monument to George Lord in Princetown churchyard.

Across the entrance to the car park at the rear of Lord's Café is **Stoneycliffe House**. Albert Bolt built his home here, conveniently next door to his shop. Above the entrance the inscription 19AB05 represents Albert Bolt 1905 (not, as it may be misread, AD1905!). Mrs Turner from Rundlestone Corner came to keep house here, and would babysit, do the laundry and cooking, and look after the family. Joshua Rowe originally leased the land (before the house was built) from the Duchy in 1810.

Bolt's Store was a Co-operative Store in 1887 and then, after being taken over by Albert and Mary Bolt, it was named The Mart and known as Bottom Shop. It sold almost everything you could want from its cold-room (cooled by a stream running through it), butcher's and drapery, with its own bakery next door. Clothes, coal, paraffin and methylated spirits were also available. Few families owned cars, and vans would deliver goods around the neighbourhood. The Bolt family also ran a farm at Prince Hall.

Mary Bolt's maiden name was Duke and her brother, Sir Henry Duke, was a barrister and President of the Divorce Courts, later ennobled Lord Merrivale in recognition of his work with the Merrivale Quarries. Albert died at the age of 46 and left Mary with the business and a family.

One of Albert's children was Greta Victoria Alexandra. The eldest son, Wesley, was 14 when Albert died, and he took over the running of the shop. He became a Justice of the Peace, a freemason, a school governor at Princetown and at Tavistock Grammar School, and he was involved with the workhouse and the prison.

Winnie Cooper, in apron and hat, ran Bolt's from 1932 until 1957 and again in 1963 for a few weeks during the bad winter. She earned five shillings a week, working from 8a.m. to 10p.m. A clome jar kept the milk from going sour as refrigerators were not available and a meat safe preserved the meat. The cheese was protected by muslin. Sausages and dripping were made on site and deliveries to Postbridge, Merrivale, Hexworthy and other neighbouring areas undertaken. Bread was delivered to the prison. The storage of grain, for baking, and of cattle food, ensured that rats were plentiful; the rodents would even eat the Sunlight and Lifebuoy soap which was wrapped in paper!

Sugar and biscuits were weighed and packed in blue or greaseproof paper tied with string, not pre-packed. Broken biscuits were sold cheaply and Mrs Bolt, when working alone, was too generous for there to be much of a profit. She was able to provide margarine without coupons or points during the Second World War and this added a new dimension to the meals of those prison officers who were housed in the Duchy Hotel opposite.

Despite being isolated in the middle of Dartmoor, the women of the town could buy the latest fashions from Bolt's, which were sent from Cooks in London and replenished regularly with more up-to-date

Duchy Square with The Railway Hotel on the right and A. Bolt, grocer, on the left. **(DG)**

Lord's Cafe. (RJ)

Ma Bolt outside her house with Bolt's Store on the right. (DC)

Bolt's Store (right) *and house* (left). (FO)

Pony outside Bolt's Store, walking along Two Bridges Road towards Princetown Square, 1951. (HC)

A local delivery van. (DG)

Bolt's Store with ponies in the Square. (AG)

outfits. The bad winters led to an increased demand for clothes and boosted the sale of trousers to women at a time before this became fashionable.

The butcher, Mr Davey, set up on his own in the paper shop and Wesley Bolt took over the meat sales; Princetown was well served by butchers, for at that time there were three – Bolt's, Mr Davey and, in the small building adjacent to the Plume of Feathers, Sampsons. Bob Wallace was a travelling grocer. Today old bills from Bolt's may be seen at the Rock Inn in Yelverton.

Notes

1. Palmer, J., 'In the Footsteps of Eden Philpotts, An Introduction to the Novels of the Dartmoor Cycle', in *Dartmoor Magazine 58*, 2000, pp20–21.

2. Worth, D., 'A Jubilee Landmark for Princetown', in *Dartmoor News 69*, 2002, p.17.

3. Owens, M., 'On the Track of Tyrwhitt's Tramway: Part One', in *Dartmoor Magazine 48*, 1997, pp23–25.

4. Owens, M., 'On the Track of Tyrwhitt's Tramway: Part Two', in *Dartmoor Magazine 49*, 1997, pp10–11.

5. Kingdom, A.R., *The Princetown Branch*, Oxford Publishing, Headington, 1979.

6. Gerrish, T., 'Old Dartmoor Fairs. Part 4: Princetown and Tavistock', in *Dartmoor Magazine 62*, 2001, pp28–29.

7. The Prince of Wales – Princetown, in *Dartmoor News 55*, 2000, p.24.

8. Bremer, D., 'Dartmoor Chapel', *Dartmoor Magazine 20*, 1990, pp16–17.

9. Rendell, P., 'Princetown Church, Only 180 Years as a House of God', in *Dartmoor Newsletter 31*, 1996, pp13–14.

10. Rime, 'A Winter Phenomenom', in *Dartmoor Magazine 45*, 1996, p.19.

11. Redgrave, B., 'The Great Blizzard of 1891', in *Dartmoor Magazine 22*, 1991, pp12–13.

12. Greenstreet, A., 'Snow Blocks the Line! The Great Blizzard of 1891', in *Dartmoor Magazine 62*, 2001, pp12–13.

13. Turner, P., 'Princetown in the Winter of 1962–3', in *Dartmoor Magazine 17*, pp16–18.

14. Greeves, T., 'The Winter of 1962/3 – Recollections from Western Dartmoor and Beyond', in *Dartmoor Magazine 69*, 2002, pp8–10.

15. Stanbrook, E., 'William Crossing', in *Dartmoor Magazine 47*, 1997, pp6–10.

16. Groves, R., 'Roads and Tracks', Chapter 6 in Gill, C., *Dartmoor: A New Study*, David & Charles, Newton Abbot, 1977, p.200.

17. The ship was named after the popular novel of the same name by Dr Charles Lever.

17a. Sanderson, R., *The Prison on the Moor, The Astonishing Story of Dartmoor Prison*, Westway Publications, Plymouth.

18. Ridgers, C., 'Parcere Subjectis – The Early Years', in *Dartmoor Magazine 22*, 1991, pp10–11.

19. Ridgers, C., 'Parcere Subjectis – The Formative Years', in *Dartmoor Magazine 23*, 1991, pp27–28.

20. Ridgers, C., 'Parcere Subjectis – The End of an Era', in *Dartmoor Magazine 24*, 1991, pp20–21.

21. James, T., 'There's One Away.' Escapes From Dartmoor Prison, Orchard Publications, Chudleigh, 1999.

22. James, T., *About Dartmoor Prison*, Orchard Publications, Chudleigh, 2001.

23. James, T., *Dartmoor Prisoner of War Depot and Convict Jail*, Orchard Publications, Chudleigh, 2002.

24. Palmer, J., 'The Prison on the Moor', in *Dartmoor, the Country Magazine 17*, 2002, pp14–17.

25. Joy, R., *Dartmoor Prison, A Complete Illustrated History, Vol. I: The War Prison 1809–1816* and *Vol. 2: The Convict Prison 1850–Present Day*, Halsgrove, Tiverton, 2002.

26. Stanbrook, E., *Dartmoor's War Prison and Church 1805–1877*, Forest Publishing, Liverton, 2002.

27. Redgrave, B., 'Conscientious Objectors on Dartmoor in the First World War', in *Dartmoor Magazine 28*, 1992, pp10–11.

28. Greenstreet, A., Princetown Work Centre 1917–1919, in *Dartmoor Magazine 56*, 1999, pp8–10.

29. Trafford, P., 'The American Prisoners in Dartmoor 1813–1815', Proceedings of the Bristol Medico-Historical Society 1986–1990, Vol.1, 1996, pp58–65.

30. Buckingham, J., 'A War Industry in Princetown', in *Dartmoor Magazine 70*, 2003, pp22–23.

31. Jenkinson, T., 'The Red Telephone Boxes of Dartmoor. Part of Devon's Heritage', in *Dartmoor Magazine 70*, 2003, pp30–31.

32. Worth, D., 'The State of Princetown Shops', *Dartmoor News 72*, 2003, p.19.

33. Worth, D., and Rendell, P., 'Old Postcards of the Moor, Part 5', in *Dartmoor News 66*, 2002, pp20–22.

Princetown Square with Bolt's Store (centre) *and Two Bridges Road to the right.* (JS)

Left: *Dave Cooper's grandfather, Jack Warne* (left), *was the captain of Henroost Mine which closed in the 1930s. He ran the mine alone for 12–18 months and paid wages from his own money. Gilbert Hext* (right) *was a railway worker, his brother was Wilfred Hext and his son, Kenneth, became a Methodist minister in Newton Abbot in about 1996. Note the jumper held by Jack Warne and the hand drill used by Gilbert, presumably before inserting the feathers to split the stone.* (DG)

Above: *Wilfred Pickles in a 'Down Your Way' programme at Two Bridges, 1950s. On the right is Jack Warne who died in 1955.* (DG)

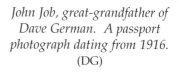

Jack Warne's grandfather. (DG)

John Job, great-grandfather of Dave German. A passport photograph dating from 1916. (DG)

Three

Rundlestone and Mistor Lane

Rundlestone is located on the road between Tavistock (6 miles to the west of Princetown) and Moretonhampstead (14 miles to the east), near the junction with the road from Princetown and one-and-a-half-miles from that town.[1] The elevation of the moor in this area makes Rundlestone (at 1,494 feet above sea level) the highest part of the highest occupied town in England.[2] It is also isolated and proved the ideal location for the quarantine of cholera victims in tents erected there in 1891.

In 1762 the Tavistock Turnpike was opened and the road from Tavistock to Two Bridges – and on to Moretonhampstead – was authorised by Act of Parliament in 1772.[3 & 4] A road from Roborough Down to Two Bridges, with a branch past the war prison, was turnpiked by Act of 1812. The tolls from the gates on this road at Princetown and Rundlestone were paltry; during a 12-month period in the early 1820s the Princetown and Rundlestone toll-houses combined were collecting only £20–£30. The Act appears to have expired, the normal tenure of such pieces of legislature being 21 years.[5] The road from the Rock on Roborough Down to Two Bridges is a more recent construction.

Rundlestone developed as a homestead for the quarrymen working at vast sites just to the west. However, more than 30 properties between Four Winds and Two Bridges have decayed, probably due to insufficient Duchy income to modernise them – a problem compounded by increased urbanisation and lack of inclination to live where services are scant.

The name Rundlestone is used in the census returns and the Duchy of Cornwall refers to Rendlestone. The origin of the name is not clear, although it may well derive from John Rundle, banker, iron founder and MP for Tavistock from 1835 to 1843, or one of his ancestors. Rundle was a member of a large and influential family and he was also involved in philanthropic activities. In 1832 he opened a dispensary at Tavistock and in 1835 submitted plans for a new Mechanics' Institute. In 1835 he suggested subscriptions for a Reading Room.

Rundlestone Tor took its name from the Rundle Stone, the only artificial boundary marker nearby apart from Siward's Cross.[6] William Crossing noted his measurement of the stone in 1881 (see page 65) but the stone was subsequently broken down to form a wall. The Rundle Stone was incised with the letter R near the top so it may be possible to find traces of it still. In 1895 Page wrote:

Nissen hut in the fields near the prison quarry. (RJ)

A snowy scene near Rundlestone.

What the Rundlestone may have been I know not, nor could I ever ascertain; (A tall stone stands by a gate in the wall near the turning to Princetown. It is inscribed with a raised R. This may be the Rundlestone, but no one in the neighbourhood could tell me what it signified) but the hamlet now bearing the name consists of a few scattered cottages which, as they approach Mis Tor, become somewhat poverty-stricken in appearance. The whitewashed walls are low and sturdy, as walls on Dartmoor must needs be; the ragged thatch is often held in place by ropes of straw or hemp, and not unfrequently weighted with stone as well. Ideas of cleanliness do not prevail among these cottars, and the space round the door would, were it not for the strong Moor breeze, be redolent of ancient vegetable and soapsuds. But look at the children. Unkempt, unwashed, their hair bleached by the sun, they are as rosy, sturdy specimens of humanity as you will see between John O'Groats and Lands End. Sumptuous fare is not theirs: bacon and cabbage, I fancy, form the staple of their rough-and-ready dinner, but Dartmoor air does the rest. Go where you will on these highlands, you will find the rising generation the same, generally dirty, mostly hatless, but pallid never.[7]

Beatrice Cresswell[8] wrote:

The few cottages we pass constitute Rundle Stone (or Rendlestone), so named from a tall boundary stone that once stood by the roadside. The cottagers at Rundle Stone call the place 'Vice's Well', and will tell you ''tis properly swampy, sure nuff.'

Almost every building here was demolished after the 100-year ground lease expired. The properties were returned to the Duchy and were deemed uneconomic due to their remote location and lack of mains services.

Mistor Lane runs north from Rundlestone, immediately west of the Rundlestone Bungalows, with the Duchy boundary to its right. At least three farms and two smallholdings were once situated on the track and the first property reached on the left, or west, side is **Ann Eva's House**, the land belonging to which is enclosed by a stone wall. To the south is a track leading to the cart sheds, used to accommodate the horses and carts (but which probably served as a dwelling in earlier years), and from this track extends another that joins with the main road.

The Eva family included Eli, Charlie (who grew a beard), Bert, Sam, Will, Daniel and Ann. Bert was a bright man, a clerk at the prison, and Daniel worked at the sandpit at Greeny Ball, the old name for Long Plantation, where he dug sand for the roads which he took away by horse and cart. Samuel was a good cook and an adept photographer; he took the identification photographs at the prison which, after his death, were disposed of down the mine shaft at Peat Cot at the Duchy's suggestion. The Evas cracked stone to provide hardcore for the roads.

The road begins to climb from Ann Eva's House and leads to a track running west opposite the remains of Mount View leading to **Mistor Cottage**, which may originally have been two dwellings. Sidney and Clara Hext lived here. Sidney was a stonemason at Ingra Tor, Swell Tor and then at Merrivale and he worked the stone for Castle Drogo and the new wing of Buckfast Abbey.

The late Bernard Hext was born at the cottage. He worked in the bakery and then at Merrivale Quarry, subsequently moving to the railway, on which he spent 16 years, at Kelly Bray, before another 27 years' employment at the prison. The family moved to Red Cottages at Foggintor, then to 14 Council Houses in Princetown whence Clara walked to Ivy Cottage to clean for her mother Selina. In 1945 the family moved to Blackabrook Farm.

The road north continues alongside the prison farmland and on to Little Mis Tor and Great Mis Tor.

The return journey leads first to **Chip Hext's House**. The property's namesake was a farmer and monumental mason who kept cows and a pig. He also lived for a time at the Foggintor Mission Hall with his wife, Catherine.

Mount View is sometimes known as **Mistor Farm**. It was constructed on a 20-year lease but building was slow and rent payments were soon due

Ann Eva with a dog outside her cottage in Mistor Lane, pictured before the Duchy added a kitchen on the south side during the 1940s.

Ivy Cottage (left), *Great Mis Lodge* (centre), *with the ruins of Sam Pengelly's House in front, and Rundlestone Lodge* (right) *looking south from a point close to Mistor Lane, 2003.*

to the Duchy. The shippen remains with a galvanised-iron roof. Water was carried from a spring to the east of the house, close to the wall, until a concrete tank was installed which was fed from the prison fields. A pipe also carried water to Eva's Cottage which was pumped to Chip Hext's House. Another pipe took water to the pumping station and a deep well provided moor water.

Alec Youngson and his wife Pansy lived here. He worked at Grey Dawn Quarry at Merrivale but was killed after being knocked into the water by a crane operated by an Austin Seven car engine. Pansy stayed at Mount View after Alec died and she cleaned Bolt's Store where she also cooked on Saturdays. Their son, Don, helped in the shop and at about three in the afternoon went out in an old Ford van loaded with goods for Rundlestone and Hill Cottages; another van would go to Merrivale, generally carrying orders which varied little from week to week. The Youngsons moved out in 1960 and Mount View was demolished. A lane leads to a ruin close by the wall to the east.

Just before Ivy Cottage, in the field to the west, is the ruin of **Sam Pengelly's House** and, to the north, a number of outbuildings. Sam's sons were David and Patrick, and Maureen was one of his two daughters. In 1912 Pengelly's House was to be replaced by a pair of low granite dwellings; the Duchy considered eight feet to be a sufficient height for such Dartmoor properties, rather less than the Duchy dwellings built at that time at Shepton Mallet.

On 10 May 1858 Joel Williams, a stonemason, applied for a licence to build a house with gardens front and back; this he was granted, at a cost of £2.2s.0d. for 30 years, on 13 May, for a plot of 3.27 acres. His plan showed a three-bedroom cottage with three fireplaces but without a back extension. At the time of the 1861 census, Joel, who had come from Stithians (but who was possibly born in Penryn), was listed as living in the newly-erected property, which was known later as **Ivy Cottage**.[9]

Ivy Cottage was to be inherited by Jonathan Williams, son of Joel and his wife Ann (née Laskey, from Islington, London). Jonathan had been born at Walkhampton in 1848, a decade before the cottage was built, and he married Selina Ann Lord from Whitchurch. Jonathan and Selina had ten children: Louisa, Alice (mother of Peter), Clara, Albert, Mabel, Charles, Nellie, Alfred, Elizabeth and Ethel.

On 9 March 1880 Jonathan's brother, Ambrose, applied to build on land behind Ivy Cottage which had formerly been held by his father, Joel. On 19 July he was granted two acres at a fee of £2.2s.0d. and the lease was engrossed on 19 November. The new property probably became **Pengelly's Cottage**. Ambrose Williams also leased land to the east of Ivy Cottage beyond which was Rendlestone Farm.

A postcard, franked in 1909, shows Ann Eva's House with laundry hanging outside and a woman standing beside it. The cottage, apparently never thatched, was roofed with tin and panelled in pine.

Clara Lord Williams was born in 1896. She married Sidney Hext and they moved up the lane to the existing property at Mis Tor Cottage. They had ten children, including Bernard Hext and a daughter,

Ivy Cottage, August 1968. Note that the original wall around the cottage is intact, the front wall is painted white and the roof is of galvanised iron. The entrance gate to Great Mis Lodge has not yet been built. (BH)

Left: *The ruins of the cart sheds at Ann Eva's House, Rundlestone, 2003.*

Below: *The field boundary near Ann Eva's House, looking south down Mistor Lane, 2003.*

Left: *The ruins of the west side and rear of Ann Eva's House looking south from Mistor Lane, 2003.*

Main image: *View of Great Mis Tor with the road from Rundlestone northwards. The dwellings are Ivy Cottage (right of centre) and Pengelly's House (centre) from which a track leads to Ann Eva's House (centre left) and Mount View beyond. Chip Hext's House is to the right of Youngson's, and Mistor Cottage, where Bernard Hext was born, is far left. (RO)*

Inset: *Little Mis Tor.*

Ruins of the home of Chip Hext, 2003.

Shippen and ruins of Mount View, 2003.

Inset left: *Pansy Youngson and a pony. The privvy at Mount View is in the background.* (DY)

Below: *Mount View.* (DY)

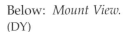

Above: *Mount View* (centre right), *with its outbuildings, and Eva's Cottage* (bottom centre). *Mistor Cottage is visible centre left and Great Mis Tor is in the background.* (BH)

Left: *Edward Perkins, Pansy Youngson's father.* (DY)

Below: *Mount View.* (DY)

The gateposts to the ruins of farm buildings behind Sam Pengelly's House from Mistor Lane, 2003.

Left: *The Hext family outside Ivy Cottage. Left to right, back row: Clara, Nellie, Louise; front: Cecil, Selina and baby.* (BH)

Below: *Alf Brown with the pet goat in the field at Ivy Cottage, summer 1947.* (LB)

Below: *Olive Brown with her goat at Ivy Cottage.* (LB)

Above: *Edna (left) and Bernard Hext in the garden of Ivy Cottage.* (BH)

Right: *Olive and Alfred Brown with their son, Louis, outside Grosvenor House flats, Princetown, 1943.* (LB)

Right: *Plan of land upon which Ivy Cottage was built, showing Ambrose Williams' land to the north.*

Left: *Ivy Cottage (right) and Great Mis Lodge (left) before the conservatory was built.* (LS)

Pengelly's House (left), *Ivy Cottage* (centre) *and Rook's House* (right), *with only one Rundlestone bungalow visible.* (RJ)

Lylie Louise Hext, who married Samuel George Stephens and whose son is Les. Clara died at Lower Corndon, Chagford, on 4 October 1965.

Mrs J. Williams wrote to E. Barrington of the Duchy at Tor Royal House on 19 June 1912 to ask whether there was any objection to her continuing to draw well water from Mr Pengelly's land, as she had enjoyed it jointly for 35 years. Her husband had been delicate for some years and was ill with lung disease for which Dr Brodrick was attending. There was clearly a boundary dispute about the water-supply.

Ivy Cottage was approached from the main road through a gateway which led into a lane lined by two stone walls. Part way along the lane, on the left, was an earth closet. At the west end of the cottage was a lean-to which formed a garage with a pigeon loft above. The roof was of red-painted corrugated iron and the outside walls were painted in a light colour. The garden was attractive and walled; flowers, beans and other vegetables were grown here. The family kept a pig to slaughter at Christmas, a goldie chicken fed on maize, and Toulouse turkeys – the cock would chase the children. Selina delivered milk in churns, perhaps from the cow at the cottage.

Jonathan died on 22 March 1914 and Selina spent the remainder of her life at the cottage. She sold tobacco, cigarettes and sweets at the porch. At the east end of the dwelling a wooden extension with a galvanised roof served as a café providing lemon and orange drinks. A sign advertised Woodbine cigarettes which were popular during the war at five for a penny. Trade was good with the troops and the Woodbines were also bought for the prisoners and hidden for retrieval by working parties.

On 29 November 1924 Mrs J. Williams wrote to the Duchy on the advice of her sons in Canada to enquire about the rent of her old house. Then, in 1935, Albert, a blacksmith, returned from Canada to look after his mother, Selina, at the cottage. He commuted by motorcycle to South Molton where he

Ivy Cottage from near Rundlestone Corner, 2002.

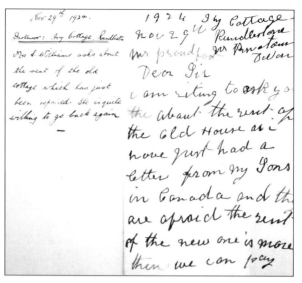

Above and below: *A letter from Mrs Williams regarding the rent of Ivy Cottage.*

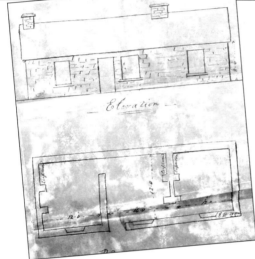

Top: *Ivy Cottage, summer 1947. A photograph by Nurse Thomas of the Royal Eye Infirmary, and her husband, Phil.* (LB)

Above: *Plan of Ivy Cottage submitted to the Duchy in 1858.*

Right: *Albert Williams on a Dartmoor tor.* (LS)

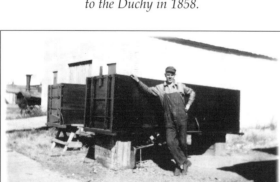

Albert Brown in Canada. (BH)

Right: *Alf Brown outside Ivy Cottage, 1947.* (LB)

Above: *Ivy Cottage* (left) *and Pengelly's House* (right) *with Nurse Forder's older sister and her son, Michael, from Bromsgrove in front, 1947.* (LB)

Inset: *Olive May Brown with Sandy the dog outside Ivy Cottage, October 1946.* (LB)

Left: *Ivy Cottage, summer 1947. Left to right: Olive, Louis and Alf Brown.* (LB)

Outside Ivy Cottage, summer 1947. Left to right: Louis Brown, Olive Brown, Mrs Taylor, Mrs Gatewood. (LB)

Left: *Michael Forder and his aunt in the garden of Ivy Cottage, 1946.* (LB)

three years as handyman at the Dartmoor Inn before he died at the age of 68.

Alf was the last occupant of Ivy Cottage and stayed there until it was condemned in May 1953 due to the lack of running water and sanitation. The lavatory was an Elsan in a shed and the tap was in the porch on the east side of the cottage. Louis' bedroom was at the west end, entered through a door in the south end of the wall. In the kitchen next door was a black-leaded stove, and the scullery, a single-roomed rear extension, was entered from the rear of the kitchen. Next to the kitchen was another bedroom and next to this, entered via an exterior door, was the tearoom. In front of the property was a walled garden and in front of that a further walled kitchen garden.

Ivy Cottage survives only by virtue of its use as a pig shed by a neighbouring farmer before it was reinstated as habitable accommodation.

worked as a blacksmith before finding employment at the council's Wilminstone Quarry in Tavistock. Albert married Alice Stephens after an engagement of 28 years and they lived at the cottage until 1946.

Selina died in 1942 and is buried with her husband, her son Alfred and their four-month-old daughter Ethel, in a single grave in Princetown churchyard. The memorial is a rough red-granite cross that bears the following inscription on its east, south and west faces:

In loving
memory of
Jonathan,
Beloved
husband
Of Selina
Williams
Died Mar. 22nd
1914. Aged 68.
At Rest.

Also Ethel
Died Aug. 1893
Aged 4 mts.
Also Alfred
Died April 11th
1928 aged 33 yrs.

In loving
memory of Selina
Loving wife of
J. Williams
Died Nov. 16th
1942
Aged 83 years,
Peace, Perfect
Peace

After Selina died Albert continued to live at Ivy Cottage until his death in 1978. He offered the deeds of the cottage to Bernard Hext who did not take them and it appears they were destroyed.

Alfred Charles Brown and Olive, parents of Louis Brown, moved from 16 Burrator Avenue to Ivy Cottage, where they lived from October 1946 until May 1953 and kept a Dexter cow. Alfred worked as a crane driver and hand driller at Swell Tor Quarry having worked at Merrivale aged 15. In 1932 he went to Swell Tor Quarry where he remained until its closure; then he spent a year at Tavistock Council Quarry before taking up night duty at the prison where he stayed for 13 years. He worked at Grey Dawn Quarry for a year around 1946 where he brought Mr Youngson out of the pit. Then from 1947 until 1962 he was on night duty at the pumping house. He spent

Notes

1. Crossing, W., *Princetown, Its Rise and Progress*, Quay Publications, Brixham, 1989.
2. *Bell's Pocket Guides*, Devon, 1929.
3. Groves, R., 'Roads and Tracks', Chapter 6 in Gill, C., *Dartmoor: A New Study*, David & Charles, Newton Abbot, 1977.
4. A notice appears in the *Exeter Flying Post*, 8 May 1772, p.3a, noting the Merrivale to Cherrybrook Road.
5. Groves, R., 'Roads and Tracks', Chapter 6 in Gill, C., *Dartmoor: A New Study*, David & Charles, Newton Abbot, 1977, pp196–200.
6. Martin, E.W., *Dartmoor*, Robert Hale, London, 1958, pp53–54.
7. Page, J.L.W., *An Exploration of Dartmoor and its Antiquities with Some Account of its Borders*, 2nd Edition, Seeley and Co., London, 1889, pp140–1.
8. Cresswell, B.F., 'Dartmoor with its Surrounding Map', *The Homeland Handbook, Vol.VIII*, Covent Garden, p.68.
9. Brewer, K., *The Railways, Quarries and Cottages of Foggintor*, Orchard Publications, Chudleigh, 1999.

Monument to Jonathan Williams and his family in Princetown churchyard.

FOUR

⸙⸙⸙

FROM RUNDLESTONE TO FOUR WINDS

The hilly road from Rundlestone drops downhill towards Merrivale before continuing on to Tavistock. During the blinding blizzard of 1963, and despite chains being attached to the wheels of the vehicles, the road was impassable. Cecil Frampton, a tough man with experience in the Royal Horse Artillery in Rawalpindi in 1926, and Mr Cooper, drove down from the prison farm to collect a prisoner and two escort officers from the Dartmoor Inn at Merrivale. A caterpillar tractor and trailer (the occupants of which were covered by tarpaulin) was needed to make the journey across the moor. Arthur Smith, who hitched a lift on his way back from work in Tavistock, recalled the sudden change from sunlight to pitch black at Moor Shop.

Soon after the left turn from the Princetown road is another turning on the left to **North Hessary Tor transmitter**, followed by a weather station and telephone box. Farm buildings further along the road stand on the site of older houses, one of which is known as **Harriet's House**. Further up the hill were two properties, inhabited in the 1850s by the Eva and Hext families.

In 1852 William Eva had a double thatched cottage here. By 7 March 1884 **Jane Eva's cottage** was

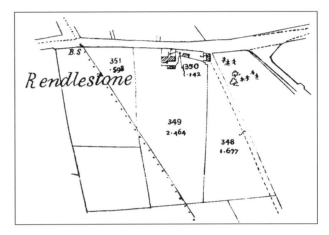

A plan of buildings east of Ru(e)ndlestone Lodge, 1850s.

said to be dilapidated and the fields not manured. On 3 May 1884 the property was deemed unfit for human habitation by the Tavistock Union Rural Sanitary Authority and the inspector wrote of the:

...deplorable state of the leaseholder under the Duchy (Jane Eva) at the time of my visit. She was in a most filthy state – clothing a mass of rags – dress unkempt, and an old blanket with holes in it to cover herself. I am informed there is not any bed and the premises are unfit for habitation. Could you enter on the premises and get them (she and her son) out without the matter coming before the board.

On 21 June 1884 Jane Eva was removed to the County Asylum and her premises were put under the charge of Mr Heddy.

This smallholding belongs to **Rundlestone Lodge**, seen further down on the left with its companion bungalow, **Great Mis Lodge**, on the right of the road. These two Rundlestone Bungalows, one on each side of the road, are mirror images of each other. The bungalows were built around 1925, probably by the Duchy, and are made of stone with a

North Hessary Tor transmitter, 2002.

MEMORIALS TO THE HEXT FAMILY

*In loving memory of
Lillie Hext,
who died
29th Dec'r 1943
Aged 51 years
Also Charles Albert
Beloved husband of
the above who died
29th April 1946,
Aged 52 years
Reunited*

*In loving memory of
Samuel John, beloved
Husband of S.A. Hext
Who died Nov. 26th
1929, aged 76 years.
"Safe in the arms of
Jesus."
Also of Susan Ann
his beloved wife who
died Jan. 12th 1944,
aged 83 years,
At Rest.*

*In loving memory of
William Hext Aged
84. Also his beloved
wife Joan Sybil
Stafford Hext
Died 2nd June 1995
Aged 69*

*In memory of my
beloved husband
Willie Hext who died
3rd June 1968
Aged 77 years*

*In loving memory of
Sidney Hext Beloved
husband of Clara and
dear dad of all his
children.
Died 5.7.63 Aged 69.
In Heavenly Love
Abiding
Also Clara, beloved
wife of Sidney
Loving mother of all
her children.
Died 4.10.1985,
aged 69.*

Above: *Arthur Smith
with Cooper the horse
pulling a hay cart at
Rundlestone, 1947.* (AS)

Right: *Susan Cooper, wife of
Samuel John Hext.* (LS)

Left: *In Princetown churchyard there are
memorials to the Hexts, a family living on Dartmoor
since the fourteenth century. The photograph* (inset)
depicts Samuel John Hext. (LS)

Above: *The marriage of George Samuel Stephens
and Lylie Louisa Hext, 1937. Left to right, back
row:* Bill and Lil Finch, Janie Palmer (bridesmaid),
Clara and Sidney Hext. *Annie Stephens* (left) *and
Selina Williams* (right) *are in the front row.* (LS)

Left: *Arthur Smith.* (AS)

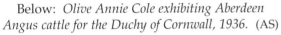

Above: *Four Princetown postmen*, left to right: *Henry Moore, Arthur Rook, Bob Finch and Harry Smith, outside the Villa on Plymouth Hill, 1947.* (AS)

Left: *John Henry Smith outside Rook's House, 1947.* (AS)

Below left: *John Henry Smith outside Rundlestone Lodge, 1947.* (AS)

Below: *Olive Annie Cole (later Smith) with a bull in Cornwall, 1930s.* (AS)

Below: *Olive Annie Cole exhibiting Aberdeen Angus cattle for the Duchy of Cornwall, 1936.* (AS)

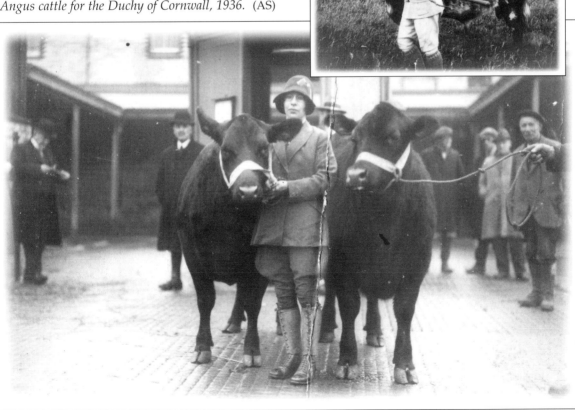

Above: *Mrs Gregory with the poultry at Beardown Farm.* (AS)

Right: *Eunice Smith feeding a lamb at Rundlestone, 1990s.* (AS)

Members of the Devonshire Regiment, including John Henry Smith, during the First World War. (AS)

The Easterbrook family outside Wheal Lucky. (FO)

cavity wall and suspended floors. They are rendered in cement.

Further down the hill is **Wheal Lucky**. The buildings here adjoin the open-cast mine to the north of the road and other workings approached by adit from the south of the road. The Hext (or Hicks) family had moved from Summerhill to Wheal Lucky[1] by 1841 and married into the Easterbrook family.

The two dwellings situated to the north of the present Wheal Lucky were home to Jane Easterbrook and Mary Jane Williams, both buried in Princetown churchyard. One property was known as Aunt Polly's.[2&3] These dwellings were East and West Wheal Lucky, the latter comprising part or all of **Wheal Lucky Cottage** where Billy Easterbrook lived with his Scottish wife, Jinny. The buildings burned down around 1900 but by 1904 had been rebuilt and the Easterbrooks continued to live there.[4] George Easterbrook walked to work in Lustleigh each week.

Quinsey Bungalow was the home of Billy Easterbrook after he returned from the town of Quinsey in the United States where he lost a great deal of money.

At the top of the hillside is **Hollow Tor** and its quarry. Lower down was **Hill 60 Quarry** where Sidney Hext worked.

Further down the hill is the turning south to **Yellowmead Farm** and the big quarries. At the roadside is a sandpit and a long walk along the old railway path to the left leads to Foggintor Quarry.

Foggintor Quarry, which is very large, has not been worked in living memory. Five quarries were

once active in the neighbourhood – Foggintor, Swell Tor, Ingra Tor, and Great and Little King's Tors. Quarrying at Foggintor was at its height between 1830 and 1840[5] and during its heyday provided employment for some 600 men.[6&7] In 1944, at the age of 43, Eric Green's grandmother died and, although she had lived near Foggintor her whole life, she did not remember the quarry being worked. At the time of writing it houses a stagnant pool of water.[8]

The impressive Big Tip belonging to Foggintor Quarry could have been the beginnings of a railway embankment. At Merrivale Quarry a similar embankment had been started, perhaps to link a line from Foggintor to Merrivale with the main Princetown to Plymouth railway. A vast quantity of stone would have been needed for such a construction. The railway from Foggintor which went past Yellowmead Farm is a possible alternative although it is not clear where that would have led.

The railway lines in the area are complicated and have branches and loops to enable the tracks to gain height from the main line at Yelverton. Today the redundant lines provide excellent territory for mountain bikes, and clearly-marked paths for walkers.

The Yelverton to Princetown railway line takes a loop around King's Tor, where two quarries were once worked, in order to gain height. Provision was made here for a proposed branch to Merrivale Quarry. The line of the loop may have been changed when the horse-drawn railway was replaced by steam. Near the line at Royal Oak was a double bungalow where George and Eliza Gibbs lived and which was later home to Alec and Pansy Youngson.

Across the hillside, Swell Tor Quarry, unlike Foggintor, has been worked within living memory. Louis Rich was a stonemason here from 1928 until he joined the Water Board in 1938; he undertook all quarrying by hand. Wooden ladders were attached to holes drilled in the granite walls of the quarry and two-inch holes, sometimes eight to ten feet deep, drilled by jumper, were filled with black powder. Later dynamite was used to bring down the faces of the quarry. Splitting stone was hard labour which, in the days before tungsten tips, would have been carried out using a star bit prepared by a blacksmith. Feather and tare was used to split stone, and long lines of splits were accomplished by muckling. The tool kit comprised a chisel, point, hammer and

Wheal Lucky House, below the site of Wheal Lucky Cottage, 2003.

Above: *The Devon County Council solid-wheeled Clayton steam wagon, outside Postbridge, early 1930s. Sam Cooper* (right) *and Bill 'Garlic' Phillips* (centre). *The wagon, which conveyed road stone from Princetown Station where it had arrived by rail from the quarries, was kept in steam over weekends at Red Cottages.* (AG)

Left: *Gilbert Hext splitting Dartmoor granite.* (LS)

Above: *Louis Brown fishing in Foggintor Quarry, 1947.* (LB)

Left: *Malcolm Gatewood fishing in Foggintor Quarry, 1947, with his father Alex, who was visiting from Liverpool where he worked in the prison service. Louis Brown is on the right.* (LB)

London Bridge at Lake Havasu City. (DG)

pitching tool and the quarrymen worked from 8a.m. to 5p.m. The 7.30 train from Princetown to Swell Tor took a convenient ten minutes. Eric Green remembered his uncle coming home from Swell Tor, which was worked until about 1938.

Many relics of the quarries abound, both on Dartmoor and in neighbouring towns. At Swell Tor kerbstones were made, 12 by 6 inches, and in varying lengths. Plymouth kerbs were harder work for they were 12 by 8 inches, four feet or more in length and bevelled. A train line ran into the quarry at Swell Tor where a dozen trucks could be held and shunted downhill with men standing on the brakes. A special train at 1p.m. on Mondays, Wednesdays and Fridays collected the trucks.

During the nineteenth century the quarries on Dartmoor provided granite for many prominent constructions such as London Bridge and Nelson's Column in Trafalgar Square. The stone was, however, too expensive for the building of the Houses of Parliament which were made using Yorkshire stone. Old London Bridge dated from 1176, although there had been earlier bridges on the site, and until 1756 the structure was topped with houses. New London Bridge, designed by John Rennie, was begun in 1825. It took 800 men more than seven years to build and the stone came from Haytor, Swell Tor and Merrivale quarries. The new bridge was opened in 1830 and in 1832 the old bridge was demolished. In 1902 the sidewalks were extended; the corbels were quarried at Swell Tor and unused pieces, made too short, still sit alongside the disused railway line. In the 1960s the bridge was found to be subsiding slowly; any increase in its width would have caused further sinking so it was decided that the bridge should be replaced. In 1968 New London Bridge was sold to the McCulloch Oil Corporation of Los Angeles for $2,460,000 and the 10,000 tons of facing stones, originally quarried at Haytor and Aberdeen, were shipped to Lake Havasu in Arizona, an area which, until 1964, had been barren desert. The bridge was rebuilt over three years and opened in September 1968.[9]

Foggintor Quarry was known locally as Hill Quarry.[10] **Hill Cottages**, demolished in 1953, may have been named after Hugh Hill of the Rundlestone Inn, who had extensive lands nearby and whose

son-in-law was a stonecutter. During the period from 1900 to 1910 the dozen dwellings at Hill Cottages were occupied by the following persons (the occupations of the men is shown):

Len and Glad Worth (council worker)
Tom and Mary Hext (stonecutter at Swell Tor, known as 'Old Tommy')
Sam and May Rich (stonecutter at Swell Tor)
Bert and Elsie Maddock (quarryman at Swell Tor)
Cyril and Rose Green (quarryman at Swell Tor)
Frank and Glad Cooper (quarryman at Swell Tor)
Aunt Sarah and Ned Mead (builder at Halfyard Brothers and then at Merrivale Quarry)
Joe and Polly Stephens (quarryman)
Bill and Lil French (quarryman)
Jack and Blanche Worth (quarryman)
Bill and Lucy Perkins (horseman for the quarry)
Bally Gould (foreman of the quarry, who resided in the big house)

Eric Green, Kath Brewer's cousin who left school at 14 and worked at Tor Royal, lived in Hill's Cottages until 1945. He recalled there being ten dwellings, a chapel and a school there. According to his grandmother the archway beneath the cottages formed the entrance to the stable. Gibbs, the postman, lived in an old quarry building beyond Hill's Cottages

After the cottages the path continues back past the site of **Rosie Eva's Farm** towards Yellowmead Farm, just before the entrance to which stone setts appear in the path. These setts would have formed sleepers for single iron chairs to secure the metal rails of a branch line from the Princetown railway; presumably an extension of the track was planned beyond this point.

Rosina Eva lived at **Rosie Eva's Cottage**, below Hill Cottages, before moving to the Mission Hall where Fred Allen was the rector. Rosie used to travel in Bolt's van which delivered bread and other goods. The cottage, now in ruins, existed in 1963 and was subsequently taken over and incorporated into Yellowmead Farm. Rosie died in 1936 and is buried in Princetown churchyard where her epitaph reads:

Hill's Cottages at Foggintor, early 1900s. (FO)

Above: *Wyn Mead outside Hill Cottages, Foggintor, 1945.* (IM)

Above: *Wyn and her son Ivan Mead outside Hill Cottages, Foggintor, 1945.* (IM)

Right: *Norman and his son Ivan Mead outside Hill Cottages, Foggintor, 1945.* (IM)

Ivan Mead outside Hill Cottages, Foggintor, 1945. (IM)

Norman Mead with a pig outside Hill Cottages, Foggintor, 1945. (IM)

In loving memory of
Rosina Eva,
Who entered into rest
28th Aug. 1936,
aged 79 years.

Also of Alice Maud Mabel
Daughter of the above
Who died 28th Feb. 1912.
Aged 16 years
Simply to Thy Cross I cling

Yellowmead Farm is constructed from moor stone and was built by George Cole's great-grandfather who worked in the quarry. George's father, a monumental mason, worked Yellowmead part-time during the First World War; at night he worked at Swell Tor Quarry and after the war he was employed by a firm at Exeter making the pinnacles for Exeter Cathedral. George farmed Yellowmead when he was the prison shepherd. He scythed the fields by hand. George's son Peter then took over and at the time of writing his grandson is there, the seventh generation of the Cole family to farm Yellowmead.

Red Cottages[11] were painted with red oxide paint, hence the name. George Cole was born at No. 6 of the 12 semi-detached cottages. From 1918 until 1920 nine of the properties were occupied by relatives of Bernard Hext:

Gran and Grandad Hext (a stonecutter who finished work at Hill Quarry aged 60)
Aunt Bess and George Mead (a blacksmith at Swell Tor)
Aunt Celia and Sam Cooper (steam engine driver for the council)
Dickie Rich (a quarryman at Swell Tor)
Albert and Kate Michell (a stonecutter at Swell Tor)

Ivan Mead outside Hill Cottages, 1945. (IM)

Aunt Hext and Albert Mead (a blacksmith at Merrivale Quarry)
Gran Cooper (mother of Gran Hext)
Bill Phillips (known as 'Garlic', at Halfyard Builders)
Albert and Beat Cole (known as 'Yobby', part-time quarryman and farmer who worked at the prison in his later years)

Westmead Quarry is some 300 yards below Red Cottages. It was opened in 1942 by Eric Green's uncles, Joseph James and George Stephens, on land rented from Lord Roborough. In 1945 Eric and his brother Gerald started work there as stonemasons. In the winter of 1947 the workers had six weeks off. The Reception Hall of Plymouth Gin was built using stone from this quarry. Joseph retired in 1956 and Eric took over and installed a diesel compressor. Donald Warne worked here with them and the quarry was used until 1966 when it became cheaper to buy stone from Merrivale. This small quarry is now filled with water, a peaceful place not often visited.

Further along the road to Merrivale was the farm at **Four Winds**. In 1914 **Foggintor School**[12-14] opened here and was known as New School. It replaced the Chapel House that had been used as a school and church in 1912 and 1913 with Miss Saunders as headmistress; she lived in the last cottage on the right-hand side. In 1934 the headmaster planted the school Christmas tree, a gift from the prison, in the garden. In 2003 it stands as a tall fir in a copse.

New School catered for 200 children, mostly from the families of quarrymen in the area but not exclusively so. Eric Green attended the school until he was six and Donald Warne was there from 1935 until 1936 when it closed. Fred Stoyle was the headmaster during the whole of the school's existence and taught the 11–14-year-olds, whilst his wife Edna taught the 4–11-year-olds. Relief teachers included Elsie

Yellowmead Farm with Foggintor Big Tip in the background, 2003.

Left: *Ruins of Red Cottages looking west.*

Inset: *Ruins of Red Cottages with Four Winds in the background among the trees.*

Below: *Merrivale stone rows with Red Cottages, the Mission Hall and the derrick of the crane in the quarry under Hollow Tor (behind Wheal Lucky) before Foggintor School was built and Westmead Quarry was opened.* (TS)

Above: *Four Winds, looking west from Red Cottages, 2003.*

Right: *Foggintor School with Mr Stoyle the headmaster.* (DG)

Below: *Ruins of Red Cottages at Foggintor.*

Above: *Foggintor School, built in 1914 and closed in 1936, was demolished by the Dartmoor National Park Authority in 1964.* (DG)

Left: *Foggintor evening school students, 1923–24. Left to right, back row: W. Rooke, J. Rooke; third row: A. Perkins, G. Mead, D. Weeks, F. Perkins, C. Rooke; second row: S. Mead, W. Cornish, F.S. Stoyle (AA, MRST, headmaster), W. Rich, S. Ruby; front: L. Rich, W. Cornish, C. Rich, N. Easterbrook. Eleven students were not included: F. Cooper, S. Rich, W. Hext, A. Mead, N. Mead, C. Jeffery, F. Jeffery, F. Rooke, R. Drunsfield, O. Easterbrook and L. Cornish.* (DG)

Above: *Foggintor School class, 1929.* (DG)

Above: *Mr and Mrs Stoyle outside Foggintor School House, 1931.* (DG)

Right: *Three badges from Foggintor School.* (DG)

Left: *Foggintor School, 1936. Left to right, back row: George Copland, Pauline Warne, Dorothy Jeffery, Betty Shaw, Ed Jeffery; middle: Eric Green, Doreen Maddocks, ?, Susan Ellicott, Dennis Martin; front: Teddy Gibbs, Kevin Elliott, Donald Warne, Alex Shaw, Gerald Rich, Jack Sargent, Gerald Green.* (DG)

Above: *Foggintor School pupils at the Merrivale Menhir, 17 May 1927.* (DG)

Vegetables grown in the Foggintor School garden, 1929. (DG)

Above: *A view of Merrivale looking east from near the old Post Office. The photograph shows Mary Ann Brown* (left) *and her younger daughter Jane* (right) *with the Dartmoor Inn visible in the centre.* (LB)

Right: *Alfred and Olive Brown outside Walkham Terrace, Merrivale, 1926.* (LB)

Merrivale Bridge, Princetown. **(RO)**

Ruby-Stephens, Charlotte Gould and Miss Lucas. The property was taken over by the American Army for workshops and lorry maintenance during the Second World War. Tents were erected in the fields for servicemen, and Dr Adamson and his assistant, Miss Cooke, who undertook cancer research in Canada, used the house. The property was demolished in 1964.

Below Four Winds on the hillside to the south the road descends past the Merrivale Stone Rows[15] to a row of ancient cottages used by the miners at **Merrivale Quarry** and **Grey Dawn Quarry**. The road passes over the new bridge, past **Merrivale Farm** on the left, and then runs uphill and down again to Tavistock. On the return journey to Rundlestone one passes Merrivale Quarry where a row of 12 houses (with six doors) provided further accommodation for the quarry workers. Next is the **Dartmoor Inn** where George Blatchford was innkeeper in 1851.

The **old bridge** is on the left. As the road climbs up the hill, the site of the Methodist Mission Hall comes into view on the north side of the road opposite the turning to Yellowmead.

The **Methodist Mission Hall** at Foggintor was built between 1885 and 1887 with capital of £10. It held 150–200 people and was initially used as a day-school and chapel. Local preachers taught there. Fred Allen, who lived in the house at the east end of the hall, served here; this was his only job and it is recorded that he did not wear a dog collar. Worshippers from Hill Cottages, Red Cottages and other neighbouring areas attended the services and magic lantern shows, most of which had a religious theme. Children attended Sunday school twice each week and Eric Green recalled that his mother, born in 1898, went there as a child to sit in the wooden pews.

Winnie Cooper's mother was born at the hall, as was Louis Rich in 1914, the youngest of ten children. Five of his siblings were born there also and the older four at Gunnislake. The house itself was positioned just to the east of the hall and joined to it by the vestry. It had a front room, kitchen, scullery, passage and three bedrooms. Like the hall it was finished in varnished pitch pine. It was the only house locally to boast a flush toilet, which was operated by bucket and water from the clean spring outside; the effluent was piped into the river.

Louis' father was manager of Merrivale and Swell Tor quarries where the original house allocated him was too damp. When local preachers were not available, Louis' father, who knew his Bible well, would preach. Nelson Easterbrook, from Wheal Lucky up the hill, also conducted services there. Chapel was held in the morning and evening, with Sunday school in the afternoon. Children would walk along the road from Princetown singing hymns and Peter Bolt recalls the harvest festival, the gospel song 'Bringing in the Sheaves', the refreshments and the sale of the harvest offerings.

The hall was last used during the Second World War when Jack Bailey, foreman for the roads, lived there; it was later taken over by the United States Army. Tommy Hext and his daughter Kathleen moved to the house from Red Cottages. The Mission Hall closed and was used as a dwelling until it was demolished around 1967. The rubble was taken to Devil's Bridge on the road to Yelverton.

Between the Mission Hall and the pumping station, just up the hill to the east, are two reservoirs (now redundant), originally made out of wood with asphalt linings. Each reservoir held 40,000 gallons and was filled by three springs. Water is collected in a tank near Mount View and another near Ivy Cottage, whilst a third pipe collects water from the adit of **Wheal Lucky Mine**. These pipes meet in a collecting chamber north of the pump house. Excess water is dispersed under the road from the collecting tanks behind the pumping station and overflows into the Pilla Brook and thence to the Walkham.

Merrivale Bridge. (RO)

Above: *Merrivale Bridge looking west.* (RO)

The Falklands War Memorial, dated 14 June 1982, awaiting transfer from Merrivale Quarry. (AG)

Above and left: *The Foggintor Mission Hall on the Merrivale Road was demolished by the Dartmoor National Park Authority in 1967. It had been started with capital of £10 in 1885 and was closed in 1940. The building was owned by the Maristow estate and was in a deplorable condition before its destruction. It stood unused for 27 years. The pump house can just be seen behind the hall (above).* (DG)

Above: *Amy and William Rich outside
2 Moorland View.*

Above right: *William Rich reading the Bible in
the Mission Hall.* (LR)

Right: *The ruins of Foggintor Mission Hall,
looking west, 2003.*

Left: *Princetown waterworks, looking north-west.*

Below: *Merrivale Bridge before the new road
was built.* (DW)

Top: *Alf Brown at the old pumping station, 1948.* (LB)

Above: *Princetown pumping station, 2003.*

Left: *Alf Brown* (left) *and Bob Ellis outside the old pumping station with its asbestos roof, October 1953.* (LB)

Above and left: *Adit to Wheal Lucky Mine just north of the road from Rundlestone to Tavistock.*

Louis Rich outside the new pump house, c.1960. (LR)

The new pump house, c.1960. The building was completed in 1939 and is shown here with the extension and granite outer walls made by Louis Rich. (LR)

Rundlestone waterworks, looking north-east, 2002.

Rundlestone waterworks, 2003.

Before the completion of **Princetown pumping station** in 1939 most houses shared a well, some 20 or 30 feet deep. Billy Easterbrook was the first attendant at the station, followed by Alf Brown, the uniformed night watchman at the prison. The Plymouth City Waterworks then took over with Louis Rich as attendant. During the cold winter of 1962–3, Louis walked the two miles each way to start the pumps with his stepson, Eric Cruse, who took over when Louis retired.

There was a main pump, a stand-by, and a compressor to aerate the water through some 100 'mushrooms', whilst a smaller building housed the treatment works where lime was added. The water was filtered through chippings and then pumped up to the collecting tanks at Rundlestone.

The pumping station closed in 1991 and became derelict and the water is now channelled overland and down the hill, eventually arriving at the River Walkham. At Dousland the water is purified and mixed with Burrator water before being pumped up to Princetown and then across North Hessary Tor to Rundlestone. The pumps at Dousland are controlled automatically by radio signal from Rundlestone and a pump has been installed to raise the pressure at the Rundlestone properties that used to suffer when the tank levels were low.

The prison received water from the prison leat and drinking water from a pipe installed in an adit in the second field above Ivy Cottage until 1998.

The adit to Wheal Lucky Mine, hidden in the field to the north of the road, is enclosed behind iron doors. It is situated in the south end of a gulley and extends under the road and far into the hillside. Fine white quartz residue in the area suggests that this mineral was plentiful underground here, but by 1930 work had ceased. George Easterbrook explained that sufficient gold was mined here to make a coronation ring, perhaps for King Edward VII, in 1901.

Further up the hill to the east is **Mistor Lane**. Just before reaching this, in the field to the north and not far from the corner, a searchlight was fixed to a concrete base during the Second World War. This illuminated German planes returning from the bombing of Exeter in 1942.

The boundary of the Maristow estate with the Duchy lands is marked by a series of granite stones reaching across the hillside. In 1881, the boundary line of the forest was in dispute; the present line passes from North Hessary Tor through Rundlestone Tor to Great Mis Tor, through some of the workmen's cottage land. Other boundary stones to the south-east of Mis Tor indicate the prison's water supply and the boundary of the prison's land. Milestones appear on the roadside.

The Duchy built **Great Mis Lodge** probably in 1925 on the corner of Mistor Lane and at an altitude of 1,460 feet. The land had not been built on previously and toll-houses were not established in this area. **Ivy Cottage** is behind the lodge.

On 21 August 1925 W. Palmer took a three-month lease of the lodge at a cost of £6.10s.0d. and asked that the Duchy erect a coal-house and fence. By 15 January 1926 a flush lavatory was in use. Mr Palmer was granted Government quarters in Princetown in August 1926 and he left the bungalow on 31 August 1926 for the sake of his wife's poor health. The next occupant was probably Miss White who was followed by Mr and Mrs Bray (he worked in the prison) before Jack R. Worth and his wife moved in. Bessie Forder wrote from London and took over the

Left: *The Hext family beside the east wall of Great Mis Lodge before a porch was added in the 1950s. Ivy Cottage is in the background to the right with its lean-to garage, pigeon loft and outbuildings.* Left to right: *Lylie (far left) in the arms of her mother Clara, Selina (Clara's mother, Gran Hext) with Cecil in front, Nellie, Sidney (with his pipe).* (BH)

Right: *Great Mis Lodge under reconstruction after the roof burned down. Note the rear extension, since replaced by a conservatory.*

Above: *Nurse Forder's sister's son Michael (right) and Louis Brown with Rook's House in the background, June 1947.* (LB)

Above: *Nurse Forder's sister sawing wood outside the garage at Great Mis Lodge with Alf Brown, 1947.* (LB)

Above left: *Nurse Forder (centre) and her husband, Ken (behind), celebrate her retirement from nursing in the Town Hall, 1960.* Left to right: *Thurza Cribbett, Leonard Worth, Edna Callow, Ivy Worth.* (LC)

Left: *One of three pet goats with Louis Brown and Michael (right), 1940s.* (LB)

Left: *Great Mis Lodge with Ivy Cottage* (behind) *with its galvanised roof. Mrs Ellis is with the Dexter cow from Whitchurch, called Shillington Pat, 1948.* (LB)

Below: *Rook's House from the garden of Ivy Cottage with Olive Brown* (left) *and Maureen Ellis, April 1953.* (LB)

cottage on 29 September 1926; in 1927 she asked that the living-room range be moved to the scullery.

Until the mid-1990s generators provided power and for many years oil-lamps were used for light. The Lodges and Ivy Cottage were finally joined to the mains when cables were run from the transformer at the north end of the path to the North Hessary transmitter. 'Gran Forder' and his son Ken lived at the lodge. Ken married Daisy, the Catholic District Nurse, who did not want to live in the town and was known to walk into Princetown with her midwifery bag day or night. A garage was built for her Morris Minor car which she used to cover the district. The Forders ran a café in their front room where tea, Mars Bars and appropriately-named rock buns could be purchased. This was known as 'The Highest Café in England'.

Rook's House was a large four-bedroomed property situated to the east of Ivy Cottage in its own field. The earliest mention of this dwelling appears on 1 April 1891 when a licence was issued to rebuild the cottage and buildings which had been situated there previously. On 29 September 1891 W.J. Rook's lease was extended from 41 to 60 years.

A solid but compact house, Rook's was never thatched. On entering the porch, the living-room was to the right with the scullery behind, and on the left was a bedroom with the dairy behind. The first floor had bedrooms, to the left and the right, and there were two staircases, front and back.

Three spinster sisters, Ellen, Bess and Minnie Rook, occupied the property with their two brothers, one of whom, the postman and cobbler Arthur, was known as 'Snobby'. Local boys used to tie a button to a string and attach the string to the window frame with a drawing pin so that when the wind blew, it sounded as if someone was tapping outside.

Charlotte Rook, Gladys Williams' aunt, used to bicycle down to Blackabrook Farm. In Princetown there are several graves of members of the Rook and Rooke families:

*In loving memory of Francis Albert
beloved husband of Susan Ann Rook
who died March 2nd 1934, aged 70 years
"Missed by All"
Also of Susan Ann,
Loving wife of F.A. Rook
Died 24th Feb. 1951, aged 86*

*In loving memory of
Samuel Rook who died May 3rd 1978 aged 82
Rest In Peace*

*In ever loving memory of Mary,
The dearly beloved wife of David Rook
Who departed this life March 30th 1917,
Aged 37 years.
Peace Perfect Peace
Also of David
Her beloved husband
Died June 18th 1951, aged 93 years
God bless them, we miss them*

Fire at Great Mis Lodge. (LC)

Just beneath this stone are deposited
The mortal remains of Sarah Rook
Who died the 4th of March 1868,
Aged 62 years
An affectionate wife, a tender mother and a
sincere friend to those who knew her.

In loving memory of William Rook
Who died Jan'y 6th 1913
Aged 82 years
Though death divides,
fond memory clings
Also Jane, wife of the above
Who died Feb'ry 3rd 1914
Aged 80 years
After toil, comes rest

In loving memory of James Rook,
Who died Feb 6th 1891,
Aged 63 years.
Also Maria, wife of the above
Who died Sept'r 9th 1878
Aged 41 years
Why do we mourn departing friends,
or shake at death's alarms
'tis but the voice that Jesus sends
to call them to his arms

Notes

1. Price M., 'The Story of Charles and Charlotte Ann Easterbrook', in *Dartmoor Magazine 42*, 1996, pp6–8.
2. Price, M., 'Two Old Ladies of the Moor, Part I: The Story of Jane Easterbrook', in *Dartmoor Magazine 19*, 1990, pp22–24.
3. Price, M., 'Two Old Ladies of the Moor, Part II: The Story of Mary Jane Williams', in *Dartmoor Magazine 20*, 1990, pp10–12.
4. Brewer, K., *The Railways, Quarries and Cottages of Foggintor*, Orchard Publications, Chudleigh, 1999.
5. Woods, S.H., 'Foggintor Quarries', *Dartmoor Stone*, Devon Books, Bovey Tracey, 1998, p.283.
6. Brewer, K., 'The Foggintor Area, Part 1', in *Dartmoor Magazine 6*, 1987, pp3–6.
7. Brewer, K., 'The Foggintor Area, Part 2', in *Dartmoor Magazine 7*, 1987, pp3–6.
8. Jenkins, C., 'The Pool That Was Once a Hill', in *Dartmoor, the Country Magazine 5*, 1999, pp56–58.
9. Elmer, C., *London Bridge in Pictures*, Scottsdale, Arizona, 1983.
10. Brewer, K., *The Railways, Quarries and Cottages of Foggintor*, Orchard Publications, Chudleigh, 1999, p.119.
11. Brewer, K., 'The Foggintor Cottages', in *Dartmoor Magazine 23*, 1991, pp24–26.
12. Stevens, B., 'School in the Middle of Nowhere', in *Dartmoor Magazine 12*, 1988, pp20–21.
13. Stoyle, I.F., 'Memories of Life at Foggintor School House', in *Dartmoor Magazine 14*, 1989, pp8–9.
14. Stanbrook, M., *Old Dartmoor Schools Remembered – 1*, Quay Publications, Brixham, 1991.
15. Walker, J., 'Merrivale's Double Stone Rows', *Dartmoor Magazine 71*, 2003, pp22–23.

The old cattle grid looking towards Rundlestone Corner. (RJ)

FIVE

FROM RUNDLESTONE TO TWO BRIDGES

The road from Rundlestone Corner to Two Bridges passes several ruined dwellings. On the northern side the road runs down the edge of Far Rundlestone Field (to the north) and then past Battam's Field to a gate where the old track to the moor was used to bring peat to the naphtha works at the prison. This embankment was the foundation for the tramway and iron rails were once plentiful here – now they can be seen in the area in the form of posts for wire fencing.

Leading from this point also is the path to **Fice's Well** or Vices' Well where a stone commemorates the millennium. A second stone, marked

Looking east to the ruins of Summerhill near the trees (centre), 2003.

with a cross, is set in the ground to the east of the prison leat and marks the point where Cyril Edward Sinclair, leat man from the prison, was killed by lightning on 6 July 1983 whilst carrying out his duties on the prison leat. Nissen huts were sited here during the Second World War and were used to house service personnel before the D-Day landings in 1944.

Further on, past the site of an old quarry, is the plot of **Summerhill Farm**. Before the Second World War the Misses Smith lived at the smallholding where they kept three cows in a field also called Summerhill. The Smiths ran a tearoom which served scones, bread, jam and cream. Harry Watson and his son, Ken, leased the farm after them and it was later demolished. Water from the well outside Pascoe's Cottage ran under the road, through two fields, to a well at the back of Summerhill Farm.

Further down the hill and just before the river is the ruin of Blackbrook or **Blackabrook House**. Jack Worth lived here and Sam Pengelly also moved to the dwelling from his house at Rundlestone. A barn was situated behind the house in Spring Field. Entrance to the house from the road was up a short drive and into a lean-to or back-house that formed the scullery. A bench seat in front of the window and a long table and two armchairs furnished the kitchen-diner that was two steps up from the scullery. Upstairs there was one bedroom to the left and two more to the right. Water was obtained from a well on the west side of the river, some 60 or 70 yards down the hill. Jack Worth, the Cooper family and the Hexts lived here too. American soldiers passing by in lorries during the Second World War threw apples and sweets to the children on the roadside.

After Blackabrook House is **Blackabrook Bridge**. The river used to yield plentiful salmon that were salted and hung for the winter and also fed to pigs on the farm. In the 1920s salmon were abundant in the rivers and 5,000 fish were netted one year at the Dart estuary. In December salmon still spawn in the higher reaches of the Blackabrook where prison working parties used to clear the spawning grounds.

Higher Watern or **Blackabrook Farm** comprised 249 acres of land, originally leased by the Duchy to William Brough. The Rook family built Blackabrook Farm, a smallholding with two fields. It was not as

Above and top left: 'Swifty' Fernley Warne. The image above was taken beside the West Dart River. (DG)

Left and below: 'Swifty' Fernley Warne, water bailiff, who died in 1976 aged 64. (DG)

The Hext family in front of Blackabrook shippen, 1950. Left to right: *Eric (with the Welsh Collie, Floss), Les, Clara (feeding the pet lamb from a bottle), Bernard and Billy* (in front). (BH)

Inset: *Dartmoor ponies at Blackabrook Farm.* (DC)

good a property as Summerhill. It was two houses joined by a lean-to porch, the Rooks occupying the western part and the Coopers the eastern. Henza and Myra Cooper, Margie Williams and her sister Gladys, known as 'Cheel' (the local term for the youngest child), lived here. When the Coopers moved out they were succeeded by the Hexts. In 1956 Ken and Hilda Watson moved to Blackabrook Farm. Although the interior was plastered and papered, the property was damp, a condition worsened by road repairs that led to water from the road being channelled into the well. The Watsons moved to Middle Merripit in 1959 and then to Greyhound Farm at Postbridge. Thereafter the farm was taken

over by the prison and was eventually pulled down in about 1960.

Gladys Williams was born at Blackabrook Farm and her parents died at Oakery Crescent. She walked to school through the prison fields and along the walls. Her father, Henry Cooper, had two cows and Gladys would carry the milk up to Rundlestone on alternate days. Henry, who was employed by the prison, patrolled the walls on horseback.

Blackabrook Field behind the property is a long rectangular field that extends right up to **Long Plantation** except for a small area at the east end known as Leg of Mutton. Nissen huts were erected in the fields for servicemen in wartime.

Gladys Martin (left) *and 'Cheel' Cooper at Blackabrook Farm, early 1940s.* (DC)

Marge (left) *and 'Cheel' on motor bikes at Blackabrook Farm, early 1940s.* (DC)

Above: Left to right: *Doris, Clarry and Gladys Cooper at Blackabrook Farm.* (DC)

Above right: *Henry and Myra Cooper who lived at Blackabrook Farm.* (DC)

Right: Left to right: *Clarry, Henry and Margaret Cooper at Blackabrook Farm.* (DC)

Left: *Herbie Cooper at Blackabrook Farm.* (DC)

Above: *Two members of the Hext family outside Blackabrook Farm.* (BH)

Left: *The Hext family at Blackabrook Farm, 1954. Aunt Doris is on the far right and David* (left) *and Shirley are in the doorway. Left to right, front:* Sidney, Bill, Sybil (Bill's wife) and Clara. (BH)

Bill Hext and his wife Sybil. **(LS)**

Above: *Blackabrook Farm. Left to right: Brian Cooper (Mickey), David Cooper (Curley) and Ann Grigg (née Warne) from Beardown Lodge.* (DG)

Inset: *Henza Cooper at Blackabrook Farm.* (AG)

Left: *Clara (left) and Sidney Hext.* (BH)

Left: *The harvest field at Blackabrook Farm, Sunday 30 July 1941. Mrs Rook (right) with Gladys Cooper on her left holding Brian. Myra Cooper (middle row, right), Winifred Warne and her daughter Ann (on the right). Herbert Cooper (middle row, left). Left to right, back row: Henza Cooper (Harry James) holding the rake, Doris (his daughter) and Gladys (her sister); middle front: Marge Williams. Herbert and his wife Gladys are also pictured.* (AG)

Right: *Clara Hext (left) and Albert, 1908.* (BH)

Left: *The Hext family at Blackabrook Farm. Left to right, back row: Bernard, Ron, William (Bill), Chip (Sidney's uncle), Sidney; front: Roy, Edna, Isabel (Issy), Clara, Gwen (Clara's daughter), Les (Lylie's son).* (BH)

Left: *Sharp the dog on the wall at Beardown Farm.* (AS)

Below: *Sarah Jane Gregory at Beardown Farm, early 1920s.* (AS)

Far left: *The wobbly-wheeled tractor at Beardown Lodge, 1989.* (AG)

Left: *Francis Cooper at Beardown Farm.* (AS)

Geese at Beardown Farm. (AS)

The Cooper family at Beardown Farm. (AS)

Left: *The back of Beardown Farm.* (AS)

Inset: *Beardown Farm.* (AF)

A field gate. (AS)

Left: *Cecil Maurice Frampton near Two Bridges. Cecil came to Princetown in 1932 as a gardening instructor and later became farm manager. The farm manager's house was opposite New Villas and behind the Catholic church.* (RF)

Above: *Beardown Lodge from the air.* (AG)

Above: *The old Devon longhouse at Beardown Farm.*

Left: *The old turf shed at Beardown Farm.*

Right: *On the load is George White and, left to right, Cliff Waycott, aged 18 years, Mr Ball, Martin Pascoe.* (DG)

Below: *Peat drying in the Dartmoor air.* (DG)

The main road near Two Bridges. (AS)

Above: *George Stephens cutting turf peat ties. George lived at Powder Mills. One 'journey' of turf was 40 yards and, when dry, constituted one cartload. Some 30 or 40 cartloads comprised one year's supply for a small farm. The tie was 20ins deep, 2ins thick and 7ins long. Some 1,440 turfs per day would produce 2s.6d.* (DG)

Left: *Cowsic River, Two Bridges.*

Above left: *Work began on the construction of the new road at Two Bridges in 1931. Princetown is to the left of this 1932 photograph and the old bridge can be seen in the foreground.* (DC)

Left: *A military camp at Two Bridges during the First World War, before Long Plantation was developed.* (TS)

Below: *Cherrybrook Farm on the main road from Exeter to Moretonhampstead and Princetown provided 'excellent board, residence or bed and breakfast'.* (DG)

PRINCETOWN, Dartmoor
Cherrybrook Farm
On Main Road Exeter-Moreton Hampstead and Princetown
EXCELLENT BOARD RESIDENCE OR BED AND BREAKFAST
Garage and Parking Good Fishing and Hunting
Own Farm produce. Highly recommended
MRS. DAWE

Watern Cottage or **Hatch's House** is a ruin on the hillside, set back from the road, some 200 yards before the conifer plantation. This was once home to the Cooper family and also, at one stage, to Mr Hatch who moved from Mistor Cottage. Fred Pengelly, Lillian's son, and his wife Rachel moved there from their cottage at Rundlestone. Rachel cleaned in Princetown and walked very fast but with a bent posture. The couple did not have children. By 1939 the house was in use as a shed and thereafter the walls were used to enclose a silage pit.

Some 200 yards beyond Hatch's House is a turning north through Long Plantation. The enormous Frank Mitchell, the 'Mad Axe-man' allegedly killed by the Kray brothers, influenced much of what went on on the prison farm. He exercised in Long Plantation by lifting heavy drums, and even a horse, but was known to cry like a child when things went wrong.[1]

Beyond the turning the road twists to the south, crosses the Devonport Leat and descends to **Beardown Lodge**. Granfa Worth, a London policeman who was well known for his good singing voice, lived in the barn (known to be as old as the Plume of Feathers) with his wife and grandson Oliver. Ann and Peter Grigg, previously of Blackabrook Farm, took over the property.

Beardown Farm dates from the late 1300s and is a Devon longhouse and a working farm. Its heyday was from 1840 to 1930, like most of the Newtake Farms, and only 20 of the 1,056 acres can be cut now. Reverend E.A. Bray held the property during the 1760s and began building an elegant Georgian Mansion just before the Saracen's Head was erected at Two Bridges in 1772. The old turf shed at the farm is of considerable age.

Moor Lodge was built in 1898 but the stable block, **Cumberland House**, is older. The road crosses the West Dart just south of the point where it receives its tributary, the Cowsic, and arrives at Two Bridges.

Trout Cottage and the road to Wistman's Wood are on the left and, up a short rise, there is the junction with the road from Moretonhampstead. The road continues to Dartmeet, past **Prince's Hall** on the right, and on to Ashburton, Holne and Buckfastleigh. The road to Moretonhampstead passes Crockern Tor (the seat of the Tinners' Parliament), Parson's Cottage, Spaders, Cherrybrook Farm and Powder Mills before arriving at Postbridge.[2] Judge's Corner, where there is barn on the south side of the road, is a reminder of Judge Buller, who built the Saracen's Head, later the **Two Bridges Hotel**. The area was known at that time for drinking, wrestling and potato selling. A horse-drawn trap conveyed people to and from Princetown. During the Second World War the hotel was used as a boys' school, albeit an unusual one with a bar selling beer and spirits to accommodate the many British and American soldiers stationed nearby.

The return journey from Two Bridges passes Colt's Fields, Park Corner and Phillips Fields on the south side of the road. Phillips Fields and Park Corner, opposite Blackabrook Farm, were once football pitches for the Borstal boys. During the Second World War Nissen huts were erected here as victualling stores for the Royal Navy.

A lane leads to **Waldron's Farm** and another to **Piccadilly sheds**; both sets of buildings were used by

Left: *A Duchy of Cornwall dinner at Two Bridges Hotel. Left to right:* Mr Owen, Hector Cribbett, Mr Mutton (in charge of the Duchy Office and father of Lesley Mutton), Captain Carter (in charge of the Range Office during the war which was situated in the Town Hall and then at Lloyd's Bank), Mrs Winnie Mutton, Mrs Stephens (of The Railway Hotel – her son Ivor ran the Dartmoor Garage and Peter had the Dartmoor Gift Shop), Ruby Perkins, Mrs Brown, Jane Stephens, Mrs Youngson (Mistor Farm), Mrs Halfyard (Ivybridge Cottage, behind the Plume of Feathers). (HC)

Above: *At the Two Bridges Hotel. Left to right: Bert Cribbett, Jimmy Stabb, Sam Pengelly, Frank Worth.* (LS)

Above: *The Harvest Festival held by Revd Reece, the vicar at Princetown, outside the Two Bridges Hotel.* (DC)

Above: *The wooden hut near Wistman's Wood at Two Bridges, c.1900.* (DG)

Right: *Horse and wood cart outside Two Bridges Hotel.* (DG)

Above: *The Duchy gave clay pipes to those who had paid rent.* Above left: *Olive Brown, Floss Halfyard, Francis Williams;* and above right: *F.H.E. Mutton, Captain Carter, Ted Owen (Duchy plumber), Les Mutton's wife, Hector Cribbett, Bob Finch (Terry's grandfather), Olive Brown.* (FO & DG)

Above: *The Prince's tenants at Princetown. Amongst the assembly at the Estate Rent Audit is Sir Walter Peacock, Secretary to the Duchy of Cornwall, who stands between the clergyman and a lady.* (DG)

Above: *The Two Bridges Hotel, on the banks of the West Dart, advertised modern sanitation, a pure water supply and four bathrooms with hot and cold water.* (DG)

Left: *Halfyards building the extension to the Two Bridges Hotel.* (DG)

127

The ruins of Pascoe's Cottages at Rundlestone, 2003.

The tramway (across centre) *which was used to convey peat to the prison to make naphtha, 2003.*

the prison for farming. During the Second World War the Navy was stationed in the fields near Pascoe's Cottage and the United States Army was stationed on the north of the road for two weeks at a time for gunnery practice.

On the other side of the bridge, Bog Field and Tree Field can be seen on the left. Next is the ruin of Pascoe's Cottage, shown on a plan of 1851. By 1857 L. Pascoe had died and Jon Rook had taken over the property. On 22 July 1861 rebuilding was in progress

with the roof being raised by one foot, lead gutters installed and slate taking the place of thatch. The cottage was a granite bungalow with a bitumen-painted slated roof, the tar being produced as a by-product from the gasworks at the prison. The house was on the left on entering through the gate, and the first room was the kitchen.

Frank Turner, a council road worker and a stoker or blacksmith at the prison, lived in the cottage and married the sister of George Stephens who lived at Powder Mills. Their son, Polly Turner, worked at Finch's delivering groceries and coal. The last occupant was Jack Labsleigh, a prison farm worker.

The following memorial can still be seen in Princetown churchyard:

In loving memory of Charles
Devoted husband of Mary Pascoe
Also dear father of Lucy, Emily and late Charles
Died Jan'ry 18th 1941, aged 75.
Loved By All. At Rest.
Also his wife Mary Elizabeth Pascoe
Died 20th Dec. 1946. Aged 85 years.

Beyond Pascoe's Cottage a shallow well is situated at the side of the road and a stone stile is set into the wall. A track from the peat-collecting areas north of the road crosses to the former naphtha works in the prison. The Rook family used the water supply from here and Minnie and Ellie each used to carry two buckets of water up the hill to their property at Rundlestone. This well might also have provided for the horses and men working the naphtha track.

Notes
1. Gale, C. and Howard, R., *Presumed Curable: An Illustrated Casebook of Victorian Psychiatric Patients in Bethlem Hospital*, Wrightson, Petersfield, 2003.
2. Bellamy, R., *Postbridge, The Heart of Dartmoor*, Halsgrove, Tiverton, 1998.

Right: *An old view of Two Bridges.*

SIX

THE ROAD TO THE EAST: TWO BRIDGES ROAD

The northern side of the road to the east, to Two Bridges, starts beside Bolt's, now named **Princetown Stores**. In 1810 James Cooper leased from the Duchy the land on which the store was built, along with a building to the east described as a bakehouse. A grassy area beyond a wall separates the stores from **Rose Cottage** and **Lamorna Villa**.

The **Dartmoor Garage** is on the site of the original old Temperance Hotel and was run for many years by the Pethericks before Ivor and Peter Stephens took over. Before the installation of mains electricity in 1947, accumulators to power wireless sets were recharged on the premises. Perkins and Petherick in Two Bridges Road, and then Mr Finch, provided the taxi service. Finch's Coaches meanwhile was run from Top Finch's Shop.

Squires Cottages is a terrace of five dwellings, beyond which lies the **Old Smithy**. Two other houses, also beyond the terrace, are some of the oldest in Princetown and were once the coach-house for the village carter. Good views of the prison, North Princetown and North Hessary Tor transmitter can be enjoyed from here. A milestone opposite the lane to Bachelor's Hall records:

> *Plymouth*
> *15 Miles*
> *Moreton*
> *Hampstead*
> *13 Miles*

Later the road crosses the Devonport Leat and leads down to Two Bridges. The return journey, on the south side, passes Roundhill House on the left.

Roundhill House was built in 1908. Jonas Coaker[1], the Dartmoor poet, inhabited the shippen where the fireplace at each end can still be seen and a

Two Bridges Road looking east with the Wesleyan Chapel on the right, 1924. The dwellings on the end of the row on the right are Duchy Cottages. (JW)

large wooden shelf once served as a bed for the children. It has been used as a cattle shed since 1908. The lane beside Roundhill House leads to **Roundhill Farm**, a large farm dating from the sixteenth century. The ruins adjoining the present farmhouse were once dwellings for the farm workers. Farming here were the Smith family, followed by the Turners.

The **sewage works** are situated between Roundhill House and the Ockery. The **Ockery**, or Oakery, was built as part of the Tor Royal estate.[2] Everything but the barn has been demolished. A woman named Eliza Kistle is known to have rinsed her fine linens in the river here during the 1860s.[3] Crossing the river on **Oakery Bridge** gives a further good view of the Devonport Leat meandering south of the old clapper bridge. A series of fields and plantations follows.

New London is a development of four semi-detached houses designed by the Duchy; originally eight were planned to provide accommodation for those working at Bachelor's Hall Farm. The name

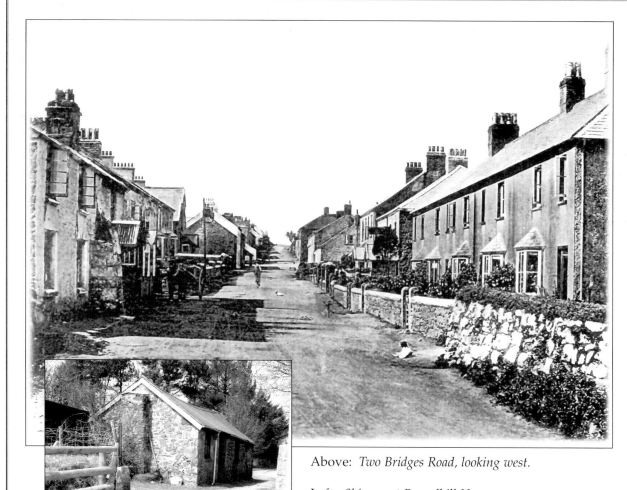

Above: *Two Bridges Road, looking west.*

Left: *Shippen at Roundhill House.*

Left: *Richard Moses holding his youngest daughter, Jean Mead, at No. 3 Two Bridges Road, 1920.* (LB)

Above: *In the garden of No. 3 Two Bridges Road, 1914. Left to right: Gladys Rapson, Richard Moses (holding Jean Mead), Gwen Mead, Phyllis Rapson.* (LB)

Left: *Williams' refreshment and boarding house on Two Bridges Road. Note the prison buildings to the right, behind the house. This is now Princetown Garage.* (DG)

suggests a style of development not in keeping with the more common arrangement of houses in terraces here. The approach from the road is through plantations, the closest being that in Windy Field and the farthest that in Misty Field.

Sunnyside is a large house, built during the 1850s, with a tenement kitchen in a working farmhouse. The shippen to the east, with a substantial stone buttress, became a garage and workshop for the cartwright with a hayloft above. Most of the 100 acres of farmland was subsumed into Tor Royal land when the property ceased to be a farm in 1981. Miss P.E. Hooker took over Sunnyside in 1923 and a decade later a man named Edward Worth moved there after his retirement from the prison service; until 1942 he ran it as a long-stay boarding house with nine bedrooms. Married couples would start their life together here whilst seeking alternative accommodation. During the 1940s it was home to 'Flash Harry', the baker at Bolt's.

Along the south side of Sunnyside is a pathway leading to Bachelor's Hall Farm. A spur from this path allowed tenants to walk to Torgate House to pay rent to the Duchy.

Oakery Crescent is a group of houses encountered along the route. By the roadside is a fountain erected by R.H. Hooker which was moved from the garden of one of the Duchy Cottages opposite the garage. It bears similar inscriptions to those found on the fountain in Tavistock Road.

Duchy Cottages is a row of three terraced cottages, situated opposite Squires Cottages. At No. 1, the home of Mr and Mrs Creber, Dr Stone from Horrabridge had a surgery.

Albert Terrace consists of nine houses, built by Albert Bolt. Miss Allen and Miss Weekes lived in the terrace and gave piano lessons to those children who were 'put to music' at a cost of seven pence per lesson – a substantial sum to a shopkeeper earning five shillings a week since it was more than a tenth of the weekly wage.

The **Wesleyan Chapel** is situated on the corner. In 1932 the Methodists here amalgamated with the Wesleyan Methodists (the earliest Methodists), the Primitive Methodists (who tried to keep the early-nineteenth-century Methodism alive), and the United Methodists (mainly Bible Christians from Shebbear in North Devon). The chapel is now a United chapel, with Church of England and Methodist services alternating. The chapel was used during the late 1980s to house families when they visited relatives in prison; the Sunday school for 160 children was at the back of the building. The annual Sunday school outing involved the whole town and some 13 wagonettes or open coaches would take the villagers on their only outing of the year to Paignton, Torquay or another seaside town.

To the west of the chapel is the road to Tor Royal, Peat Cot and Whiteworks and on the western corner

Above: *Roundhill Farm with the entrance porch visible through the trees.*

Below: *A charabanc (reg. C0 2294) outing in front of Bowden's Café, now Fox Tor Café.* (DG)

of this road is **Tor Royal Lodge** which is situated on the site of the original lodge to Tor Royal and to the south side of Tor Royal Lane. Hector Cribbett, son of Albert John and Thurza, was born and raised at Tor Royal Lodge and, until February 2003, only members of the Cribbett family had lived there. Hector, known as 'Twin', has a twin brother, William, or Bill, who used to work for W.H. Smith before being conscripted in April 1944 to work as a 'Bevin Boy' in the coal mines at Kimberley in Nottingham.

Fox Tor Café was known previously as Bowden's and the Ten Tors. A butchery was situated at the rear.

The Railway Inn was renamed The Railway Hotel and, in 1851, James Rowe was the innkeeper. Subsequently the inn was renamed The Devil's Elbow but at the time of writing it is known again as The Railway Inn.

Just beyond the inn and before the Plume of Feathers is **Ivybridge Lane**, the path to Nun's Cross Farm. The Halfyards, builders of many houses in Princetown, had premises here where they employed 30 men.

Ivybridge Lane, unfit for road vehicles, passes South Hessary Tor to the east where the remnants of an iron cross on the tor marks one point of the boundary of a parcel of land defined in 1851 and owned by the Lopes family.[4] The path continues to Nun's or **Siward's Cross** and then to **Nun's Cross**

131

Above: *The Oakery, demolished in 1924.* (DG)

Inset: *Fishing from Oakery Bridge.* (RJ)

Right: *The barn at the Oakery, 2003.*

Above: *Inscriptions on the Hooker fountain on Two Bridges Road.*

Above: *Edward Worth, tenant of Sunnyside in 1935.* (DG)

Left: *Granny Mabel Worth at Sunnyside on Two Bridges Road. The sign advertises 'Bed and Breakfast and Teas'.* (DG)

Left: *Outside the Range Office, Princetown, 1942. Left to right: ? (the Bren gun carrier driver on range duty for the day), Gunner V. Everett (officers' driver from Norfolk), Lt R.S. Fox, RA (one of two range officers, the other being Lt E. Eastick), Sam Stratford from Peter Tavy and George from Lydford (two carpenters employed by the War Department making targets etc.), Gunner Brooks (officers' batman from Lancashire).* (DG)

Below: *Floss and Jack Halfyard.* (LS)

Left: *Two Bridges Road before the construction of Albert Terrace.* (FO)

Right: *Gladys Cooper and her father, Henry, outside the Methodist Church with Bolt's in the background.* (DC)

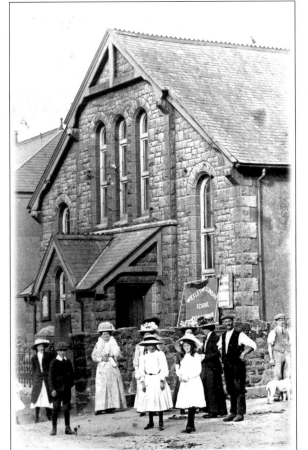

Above: *The marriage of Uncle Ernie Worth and Elsie Edwards at Embankment Road Methodist Church on 14 October 1941.* (DG)

Left: *Outside the Wesleyan Chapel.* (LC)

133

Left: *The Methodist Sunday School Anniversary Party, early 1950s. Tea was held on a Monday evening along with a sports event each June.* The front row of the head table, left to right, include: *Mrs Stephens, Winnie Cooper, Miss Allen (organist), Mr Harold Deacon (headmaster), Mrs Deacon, Mr Deacon, Edgar Rook.* (BC)

Below: *The Wesleyan Sunday school, established in 1836, 1905–10.* (DG)

Left: *Dedication of Princetown Methodist Church and Family Centre, Tor Royal Lane, 1980s.* (LC)

The Tea Rooms in Princetown, now Fox Tor Café, with the Wesleyan Chapel in the background. (FO)

Above: *The Railway Hotel, Princetown Square.* (LS)

Below: *The Devil's Elbow, 1963.* (SA)

Left: *The Cribbet family outside the new Tor Royal Lodge, 1914. The picture includes: John Herbert (grandfather), Rebecca Drusilla (grandmother, née White), and Hattie (baby).* (HC)

Below: *The Cribbetts outside the old Tor Royal Lodge. Uncle Bill* (left) *and Albert John, Hector's father* (centre). (HC)

Left: *Gran Cribbett outside Tor Royal Lodge, c.1930–36.* (HC)

Above: *Remains of a boundary marker cross on South Hessary Tor, 2002.*

Road to Nun's Cross Farm looking south, 2002. Plymouth Water Corporation (PWC) granite markers stand on the left of the track.

South Hessary Tor, 2002.

Left: *PWC post on the road to Nun's Cross Farm, 2002.*

Right: *Nun's Cross Farm.* (FO)

135

Nun's Cross Farm, 2002.

View to the west from the path to Nun's Cross Farm, 2002.

Farm[5] which is rented from the Duchy and was used by HMS Raleigh for training purposes. The farm was also used more recently by Kelly College in Tavistock. The Phillips family were the last to live there. The path continues and divides: one branch heads towards the south-east and Plym Ford and the other to the south-west and Eylesbarrow Tin Mine and Sheepstor.[6] Much of this land is on the boundary of Dartmoor Forest.

Notes

1. Greeves, T., 'The Bellever Hunt, 1875, A 'new' poem by Jonas Coaker', in *Dartmoor Magazine 27*, 1992, pp5–7.

2. Stanbrook, E., 'The Ockery', Chapter 5, in *Dartmoor Forest Farms, A Social History from Enclosure to Abandonment*, Devon Books, Tiverton, 1994, pp66–77.

3. Taber, J. and Harman, M., 'Oakery Cottage on the Blackabrook', in *Dartmoor News 62*, 2001, p.27; James, T., 'Bodies on the Moor – A Princetown Tragedy', in *Dartmoor News 73*, 2003, pp55–60.

4. On 10 August 1867 a deed enacted between 'His Royal Highness Albert Edward, Prince of Wales, Duke of Saxony, Duke of Cornwall and Rothesay, Earl of Leicester, Carrick and Dublin, Baron of Renfrew, Lord of the Isles and Great Steward of Scotland' and Sir Massey Lopes of Maristowe in the county of Devon enabled Lopes to pay £250 in order to define the land which had previously been defined by boundary in 1851 or thereabouts. The boundary was the River Walkham in the north to the River Plym in the south. The boundary line was on the Walkham at Deadlake Foot South and ran from an iron cross on the north side of the summit of Great Mis Tor to an iron cross on the east of the summit of North Hisworthy and Hessary Tor, and then to Seaward's or Nun's Cross. From there it ran to an iron cross on the summit of Eylesborough and then to a post erected at the confluence of a small stream with the River Plym on the right bank of the same.

5. Green, C., 'The Story of Nun's Cross Farm', in *Dartmoor Magazine 6*, 1987, p.22.

6. Stones, J., 'Princetown, South Hessary Tor, Eylesbarrow Mine, Sheepstor', in *Dartmoor, the Country Magazine 14*, 2001, pp30–31.

Nun's Cross or Siward's Cross, with Nun's Cross Farm in the background, 2002.

SEVEN

⤶◎◎◈

THE ROAD TO THE SOUTH:
TOR ROYAL LANE

Tor Royal Lane is a relatively recent name to replace that of Castle Lane which was given to a track leading to a beacon which was visible from Plymouth. (Tyrwhitt called the road to his house 'Castle Road' in 1785.) The road was extended later to Whiteworks and the granite gatepost above Peat Cot marks the area known as Castle Gate.

When Napoleon was threatening invasion a lookout was built of stone and timber a half mile south-east of South Hessary Tor on the ridge to Mine Cross (at the top of the hill west of Castle Farm). The moor folk called this Lookout Tor; today, only a few stones and mounds survive, much of the stone having been used to build Castle Farm. A short distance along the lane is a cattle grid and soon thereafter the site of the five-mile aerial ropeway used to convey wood from Brimpt's Plantation to the railway spur just east of the railway station where wooden sleepers can be seen. A picture dating from 1921 shows this. The engine used to power the ropeway was at Moorlands Farm.

Torgate House was built in 1895 on Duchy land as a gentleman's residence for a Mr Harris. The Duchy took it over during the First World War and the Duchy land steward lived there. A track beside Sunnyside leads to Bachelor's Hall with a spur to Torgate House. The northern extension of the house was used for offices where Duchy tenants paid their rents which had previously been taken at the Duchy Hotel and at Two Bridges Hotel where the audit dinners were held and each attendee would be given a clay pipe. The steward moved to Bath during the 1930s and now operates from Liskeard.

Tor Royal Lane, 2002.

The land steward during the First World War was Mr E. Barrington. In 1919 Mr Proudfoot came with his family to Torgate House and in the 1920s Commander Herbert lived there until it reverted to a private dwelling. Colonel Roberts of the Somerset Light Infantry (who commanded the 4th Battalion of the Dorset Regiment during the Normandy campaign of 1944–45 and who was awarded the Distinguished Service Order) let the house to General Ormsby and Major Jones. Early in the Second World War Mrs Ormsby moved to Whiteworks to allow bombed-out families from Plymouth to use the property. Torgate House was decorated with brown and green paint which was perhaps brought from the dockyard where the occupant worked. The property became vacant in 1958 and George Langton moved in in 1959.

Bull Park was built as the stud for Tor Royal Farm – the two-roomed stone building to the west was the original house. The shed to the east was the bull shed and a ring in the wall shows where the Welsh Black cattle were tethered. The house was rebuilt in 1927 and extended in the early 1990s. Two quarries provide growan (decomposed granite) as a construction

Left: *The Prince of Wales in Tor Royal Lane with John Worth (left) after a hunting trip, 1921. The aerial ropeway conveyed timber from Brimpt's Plantation at Dartmeet to the railway station at Princetown and the engine to work it was situated at Moorland's Farm near Prince Hall.* (LC)

Below: *Princetown from Tor Royal Lane, 2002.*

Above: *Digging out the snow in Tor Royal Lane, 1963.* In the background are: *Stan Cribbett, Sheila Cribbett, John Cribbett and Les Cribbett;* left to right, front: *George Williams, Leonard Worth, Olly Worth.* (LC)

Don Youngson with his 2¹/₂ kilowatt generator for Moorlands Farm. (DY)

Right: *Tor Royal Lane, February 1947.* (HC)

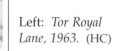

Left: *Tor Royal Lane, 1963.* (HC)

Above: *The view from Tor Royal Lane, 2002.*

Left: *Tor Royal Lane, February 1947.* (HC)

Left: *Torgate House, 2003.*

Below: *Bull Park.*

Bottom: *Bull Park.*
The original house is in the foreground.

Above: *Bachelor's Hall, 2003.*

Below: *Bachelor's Hall Farm from Torgate House, 2003.*

Below right: *Bachelor's Hall Mine, 2003.*

This page: *These images capture the landscape surrounding Bachelor's Hall, the cattle grazing on the farmland, the farm buildings and the house itself.*

Bachelor's Hall Farm, 1936. Second from left, holding a cup, is Leonard John German and, wearing a trilby in the centre of the photograph, is Uncle Bob Worth. (DG)

Tor Royal. (HC)

Tor Royal Lodge, c.1920s.
The grain store was set on staddle stones. (FO)

material for the Duchy. Other outlying Duchy buildings include the Youth Hostel at Postbridge which was built to house the Prince's polo horses. Conscientious objectors improved the old path near here from Bull Park to the mines at Hexworthy.

Bachelor's Hall Tin Mine lies close to the Blackabrook River. Quartz-tourmaline tin lodes were found here when the Devonport Leat was cut around 1795. By 1797 some 16 men were employed in the mine. Over two centuries later the shafts are collapsing but wheel pits, adits, leats and other industrial archaeological remains can be seen. The prison leat running through the land has almost been ploughed into oblivion where once it swept around the fields to irrigate and fertilise.

By 1828 the smelting house was in use as a brewery for town and prison.[1-3] However, problems in de-watering (draining) the mine eventually led to its demise; several subsequent attempts were made to make it pay before the shafts were capped in 1878.

Bachelor's Hall Farm, beyond Tor Royal, was built during the 1790s to provide accommodation for miners at Bachelor's Hall Mine and at Whiteworks. They lived at the farm during the week and returned home at the weekends, hence the name. The property was then converted into a bakery and later an abattoir. Major Harding, a writer, took it on as a private house but unexpectedly quit the building which was then boarded up. Subsequently it became an outward-bound headquarters for Plymouth School and, at the time of writing, it is used by the YMCA (Young Men's Christian Association). Some of the buildings are still employed by Tor Royal Farm.

Thomas Tyrwhitt built **Tor Royal Farm** as his home between 1785 and 1798 and at one time there was a racecourse situated here. The Plume of Feathers was constructed in 1785 to provide accommodation for Tyrwhitt's agricultural workers. Other properties nearby may be older, for example Smith

Farm at Cherrybrook. On Friday 26 September 1828 Mr George Robins advertised the auction of Torr (sic) Royal Estate in Devonshire in one lot at a price of upwards of £47,000. It included 2,284 acres in the Forest of Dartmoor with an 'admired residence' and a railroad direct to Plymouth that had been constructed two years before. The property is said to be haunted and the Beast of Dartmoor has been seen here. In 1911 Ada Kistle became a nanny there at the age of 14.[4] Lillie Langtry was said to have visited the house and Edward VIII and Mrs Simpson reputedly stayed here, the former carrying out his shopping at Bolt's.

Tor Royal Lodge, built of stone from Foggintor Quarry like Tor Royal Farm, is one of several lodges in the area built for Duchy grooms; it was probably designed by the Duchy architect, Alexander. It has four rooms, each with a fireplace set into the corner and a lean-to has been added. Edgar Williams lived here and was one of two grooms who cared for the six horses that came up from Ivybridge during the winter. He married Gladys 'Cheel' Cooper.

Above: *Tor Royal Lodge, 2002.*

Above: *Sea Bath at Tor Royal Stud Farm, 1921.* (DG)

Right: *Peat Cot hamlet.*

Above and left: *Castle Farm, home of the Worth family.* (DG)

Above: *The Worth family, 1964. Left to right:* Aunt Mabel, Aunt Elsie, Uncle Ernie, Uncle Bob. (DG)

Above right: *Hilda Worth as a baby.* (DG)

Above: *The Worth family at Castle Farm, 1953. Left to right: Ernest, Mabel and Bob.* (DG)

Right: *High tea in the Nissen hut with Uncle Ernie, Aunt Mabel and Cliff Waycott.* (DG)

Above: *Devonport Leat, 2002.*

Left: *Granny Mabel Worth (née Job). Her parents owned Harrowbeer Farm in Yelverton.* (DG)

Tavistock Rural District Council.
✱✱✱

T. H. HARRIS, A.M.I.S.E.,
Sanitary Inspector and
Building Surveyor.

TAVISTOCK,

26th Nonember 1934

Your Ref.

Dear Sir.

Milk Sample,Cleanliness Test.

I am pleased to inform you that the report on the sample of milk I took at your premises on Tuesday last,is as follows;-

B.Coli. absent in 1/10th c.c.

Count,   4,800 per c.c.

Grading,   Grade "A" Standard.

Yours faithfully

Mr H.R.Worth.

Castle Farm.

Peat Cot.

PRINCETOWN.

A cleanliness test on a milk sample from Castle Farm, 26 November 1934. (DG)

Above: *Uncle Ernie's and Aunt Elsie's home at Peat Cot. This old Nissen hut was left by the military after the Second World War.* (DG)

Above: *A horse and hay rake at Castle Farm.* (DG)

Left: *Uncle Ernie Worth and Robin with milk trap, delivering milk from Peat Cot to Princetown.* (DG)

Above: *The sign over the door at Peat Cot Chapel.*

Left: *Peat Cot Chapel.* (JW)

Above: *Peat Cot Chapel, 2003.*

Above: *Peat Cot Farm, 2003.*

Above: *Peat Cot Cottage, 2003.*

Right: *The Wesleyan Chapel at Peat Cot, 1952. The last service was held here in 1983. Left to right: Bill Halfyard, Lou Rich, Mabel Worth and William Halfyard with Leonard German in the doorway.* (DG)

The **Duchy Workshops** next door provide space for metalwork, leatherwork and printing, and a lock-up for Jail Ale, brewed at The Prince of Wales in the town. Opposite the workshops are the cottages.

At the end of the pine plantation on the road to Whiteworks, a lane leads to Snaky Bottom where American camps of Nissen huts were situated in 1944. Boys returning from Whiteworks after ferreting could exchange a rabbit or two for bananas, large tins of peaches and other luxuries.

The Devonport Leat passes through the remote hamlet of **Peat Cot** with just four dwellings, situated two miles from Princetown and arrived at via an unmade road.

Mabel Worth and her seven siblings lived at **Castle Farm**. Elsie, who never married, used to ride a bicycle to Princetown. Mabel was known for charming (healing) burns, a skill that reputedly worked even over the telephone, and was affectionately known as the white witch. Ivy Pascoe, Grandfa's daughter, scalded her hand and it healed well after charming over the phone. Edward Worth and his wife, also called Mabel, are commemorated in Princetown churchyard:

A group outside the Wesleyan Chapel at Peat Cot. (DG)

> *In loving memory*
> *of Edward*
> *Dearly beloved*
> *husband of*
> *Mabel Worth*
> *And loving dad of*
> *Hilda & Violet*
> *Who died Feb. 17th*
> *1952. Aged 67 years.*
> *Ever Remembered.*
>
> *Also his beloved wife*
> *Mabel*
> *Who died May 26th*
> *1961.*
> *Aged 83 years*
> *Loved By All.*

After a day riding bareback to collect the sheep for Peat Cot, a delicious evening meal of pigs' trotters was remembered as a local delicacy by Dave German. A telephone post was erected at Castle Farm and a cable buried two feet below the surface by hand digging. From here Ernie Worth delivered the farm milk by sledge when Tor Royal Lane was blocked with snow. During the Second World War searchlights were stationed here, near a Nissen hut. Ernie kept the hut as his home after the Second World War and in 1960 gave an escaped prisoner a cup of tea by the fire. He is commemorated in Princetown churchyard:

> *In ever loving*
> *memory of*
> *Ernest Worth*
> *Who joined the Saints*
> *on higher ground*
> *July 8th 1975*
> *Aged 89 years*
> *Perfect rest in heaven*
> *above.*
>
> *Also Elsie Worth*
> *Died October 12th 1993*
> *Aged 84 years*
> *Reunited.*

Peat Cot Chapel was built in 1912 as a Wesleyan Methodist Chapel to provide extra accommodation for the Worth family who held services in Peat Cot Cottage until that time. More extensive accommodation was needed as the congregation grew. Princetown families used to walk across the hills to attend services here on Sunday afternoons, singing as they went. Sometimes they also walked the longer distance to services at Postbridge. The walls and ceiling are boarded in wood and the gas-lamps fired by bottled gas, but the chapel is used no longer.

Peat Cot Farm or **Lower Peat Cot**, a square lodge-like residence of two acres and accompanied by several farm buildings, was the home of Cecil Worth and his wife Auntie Maud (née Coker).

Peat Cot Cottage, once the home of Jubilee Worth, is set in six acres and is about 200 years old. It has

Clifford Waycott cutting peat at Whiteworks. (JW)

Left: *The Worth family at Whiteworks.* (GC)

Right: *John Worth, farmer and blacksmith at Whiteworks and the prison, learned his trade at Walkhampton. George Cole is his son-in-law.* (GC)

Above, top, above left and top left: *The site of the old tin-mining area at Whiteworks, 2003.*

Right: *Knighton Lodge.* (RRO)

Above: *Knighton Lodge.* (RRO)

Above: *The shippen at Whiteworks.* (GC)

Left: *Henry Moore, the Princetown postman, 1950.* (AS)

Dartmoor ponies.

Left: *Fire at South Hessary House, 1979.* (RE)

Knighton Lodge had been built here in 1904 by Frank Worth on the plan of a terrace house. The north and west boundaries of the property were the Devonport Leat and water was obtained from a spring below the north-east corner of the property. Geese were kept next door and a number of stone buildings housed the neighbours' hens and the lavatory with an Elsan bucket for the Ormsbys. The Watsons rented Knighton Lodge and recall household rubbish being tipped down an open mineshaft.

Robert Ormsby bought the Knighton lease from his mother and then let it to Leonard and Hilda German. Ken Watson (renowned for his trial-winning sheepdogs) and his wife later took over the farm where two or three Icelandic ponies were also kept. The family walked to and from Princetown School down the three miles of road, although the journey was shorter across the moor. Mr Finch, who had lost an arm in the war, kept Bottom Finch's and used to give the children a lift in the van and sometimes delivered the post to save the postman, Henry Moore, the journey on his pushbike; later he too had a van.

Knighton Lodge was eventually let to the Army but they boarded the windows and dry rot set in. The slates were salvaged and used at a property at Liddaton. Then the contractors placed a charge at each corner and blew it up, but the house only shook and had to be pulled down by rope and tractor!

been enlarged by the addition of an upper storey and the water supply is derived from a spring.

Two-and-a-half-miles further down the road from Princetown is the hamlet of **Whiteworks**, close to Fox Tor Mire. Dartmoor was Europe's richest source of tin, at least during the twelfth century, and although the Cornish mines outstripped them in later years, the miners of Dartmoor were powerful enough to be almost outside the normal rule of law for several centuries. However, all output had to pass through the Stannary towns of Ashburton, Chagford, Tavistock and, later, Plympton, where the tin would be weighed stamped and taxed.[5] Tin lodes extend widely south of Princetown, as indeed they do over much of Dartmoor, and in 1808 this tin-mining area was sold with workmen's cottages, water-engine, pumps, rods and stamping mills. It became active from 1810 to 1816 but its fortunes varied thereafter and in February 1852 it was sold.

In 1868 the name reverted to White Works. Six miners lived nearby and kept a cow or sheep to provide for themselves; theirs was a dangerous job and involved using black powder for blasting which was notoriously volatile. By 1875 the White Works Tin Mining Company was thriving and cottages were built on the south side of the lane. When the company failed, before the cottages were completed, they were bought by the Home Office for married prison warders. One of the inhabitants here was Major General Ormsby who retired from the Royal Marines on half pay in 1932. A resident of Topsham, he had taken his family to Dartmoor for holidays; in 1933 they took the middle cottage of the three for a holiday and then decided to live there. The cottage at the eastern end was for the Mine Captain and it was this house that the Ormsbys moved into, tarring the outside with 'Dartmoor varnish' to protect it against the weather. The ruins of a farm at the eastern end were purchased after the war.

Miners' cottages (right) *and lodge* (left) *at Whiteworks, 1960s. Dave German lived at Knighton Lodge in 1949.* (DG)

At the far end of the Whiteworks cottages lived Grandfa Pascoe, who had an artificial leg fitted after being run over; he rented his cottage from the Duchy for 12 shillings a year and later his daughter, Beatrice, lived here with her husband John Worth (known as 'Admiral') and their two daughters. Granfa had trained as a tailor and recalled the working of the mines between 1882 and 1884 during his youth. A decision was taken that the mine would no longer be worked when the price of tin fell below 40 shillings a ton after which it would be filled in to the first station, but every now and then they would 'run away' – collapse further.

At the time of writing, three cottages survive, one of which is a family home. Guy Langton bought the top cottage in 1976 and sold it to Plymouth College in 1982: in 2003 the first two are used by that institution for outward-bound accommodation. The barn opposite the road

Inside South Hessary House, c.1910. (RE)

to the cottages was the carpenters' shop for the mine and some old mine buildings were still in use in recent years.

Getting around on Dartmoor in misty weather has always been hazardous. Uncle Fred Worth moved to Castle Farm after his wife died at Knighton Lodge and he used to collect Dave German every morning and read the rain gauge at Childe's Tomb; he had dropped broken china beside the path to guide him across Fox Tor Mire in the mist. Knighton fields extended to the end of Fox Tor Mire and there were three ways across the mire. Usually horses seem to sense unstable ground and are able to find their way through the mists, avoiding falling down old mine workings of which there are plenty hereabouts. The hunt would traditionally use the 'middle crossing'.

Once Robert Ormsby became stuck in the mud whilst rescuing a cow, and ropes had to be fetched to remove the animal. He also buried a pony which was killed there by lightning.

Childe's Tomb by Fox Tor Mires is the monument to a thirteenth-century landowner named Childe from Plymstock who, being caught in bad weather while hunting, was forced to kill and disembowel his horse so that he could shelter inside its body for warmth. Legend has it, using the animal's blood he wrote his will in the snow and bequeathed his estate to those who would give him Christian burial. A party of monks travelling from Buckland to Nun's Cross and Bovey Tracey took his body to Buckland Abbey and later erected the memorial on the moor. The occupants of Fox Tor Farm removed the memorial and used part of the cross to repair their buildings on the path up to Ter Hill. A curse prevented further growth of corn on the moor until the cross was restored to the memorial. This was duly carried out but the farm is nowadays in ruins.

The journey back to Princetown leads to a scattering of properties on the northern side of the road. **Tor Royal Farm Cottages** are two semi-detached dwellings opposite Tor Royal Bungalow, just before the road turns north to Princetown.

South Hessary House was constructed for Mr Herd, the head groom for the Prince of Wales' polo ponies in 1897. It is one of the highest houses on Dartmoor and was built with cavity stone walls. A severe fire destroyed the roof in 1979. Two trees at the entrance, planted when the house was built, can still be seen.

The stone fireplace in South Hessary House, c.1910. (RE)

Notes
1. Tin miner, 'Bachelor's Hall Tin Mine', in *Dartmoor News 71*, 2003, pp26–28.
2. Hamilton Jenkin, A.K., *Mines of Devon, Vol. I: The Southern Area*, David & Charles, Newton Abbot, 1974.
3. Atkinson, M., *Dartmoor Mines, The Mines of the Granite Mass*, Department of Economic History, University of Exeter, Exeter, 1978.
4. Taber, J. and Harman, M., 'A Nanny at Tor Royal', in *Dartmoor News 61*, 2001, p.16.
5. Titchmarsh, P.A., *Dartmoor County by Car*, Jarrolds, Norwich, p.31.

Above and right: *The Plume of Feathers, the oldest building in the town, dating from 1785.* (DG)

Below: *Another photograph of the Plume of Feathers.* (FO)

Left: *A photograph taken by George Pinkham (landlord) behind The Prince of Wales pub in 1945. The man standing on the right is Bob Finch, the one-armed postman.* (DG)

Above: *Rose Crocker, landlady, (right) plucking a fowl behind the Plume of Feathers, Princetown.* (HC)

EIGHT

THE ROAD TO THE WEST: PLYMOUTH HILL

Plymouth Hill, looking west. The cottages have since been demolished. (DG)

On the left and forming part of the Square is the **Plume of Feathers**, the oldest building in the town, known as the Plume and built by Thomas Tyrwhitt for agricultural workers in 1785. The fields behind were used as a campsite for the workmen building the prison from 1806 to 1809. Crockery and clay pipe remnants that appear from the subsoil are often found in molehills.

One of the innkeepers here was John Leger, who was listed on the census of 1851. A century later, the pub was in the hands of Jim Crocker who ran a supply establishment here, behind which was a smallholding for cows and just to the west the

shippen and hayloft, now the Bunkhouse. Hector Cribbett worked at the inn and delivered milk on his way to school, later using the Plume's horse and cart to carry victuals from the railway station to the prison. Mr Crocker also owned a Ford lorry, which was garaged behind the pub, and this was used to deliver goods to the Naval Store situated in Nissen huts on the site of the present Blackabrook Avenue where officers were stationed to avoid the heavy bombing in Plymouth. Mr Crocker died during the summer of 1966 and his wife, who was to pass away in November the same year, offered Jim's wagon and coal sacks to Hector.

Lodges on Plymouth Road with a Nissen hut (top left). (RJ)

Above: *Hector Cribbett's parents, Albert and Thurza, in the snow.* (HC)

Hector Cribbett's lorry snowed in behind the Plume of Feathers, 1978. (HC)

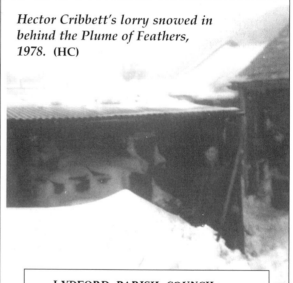

Left: *Hector 'Twin' Cribbett's twin brother Bill as a 'Bevin Boy'.* (HC)

LYDFORD PARISH COUNCIL

Chairman:
Mr. J. BELLAMY,
The Post Office,
Postbridge.

Clerk:
Mr. R. J. ALP,
Grimstone Lodge,
Horrabridge,
Yelverton, Devon.
Tel.: Yelverton ???

10th March, 1963.

Dear Mr. Crocker,

At a meeting of the above Council held recently I was asked to convey to you the sincere appreciation of my Council of the outstanding work of Mr. Cribbett during the recent period of extremely severe weather. His willing and determined efforts were mainly responsible for residents being able to secure sufficient fuel to carry them through. For him, no praise is high enough. Perhaps you would be good enough to inform Mr. Cribbett of the thanks of those he serves.

Yours sincerely,

Clerk of the Council.

Mr. Crocker,
Coal Merchant,
Plymouth Hill,
Princetown,
Yelverton.

Above: *Plymouth Hill, 1963.* (HC)

Above: *The clerk of Lydford Parish Council, Mr R.J. Alp, commends Mr Cribbett for his outstanding work during the severe weather in 1963. Mr Cribbett made sure that residents had enough fuel to carry them through.* (HC)

Above: *Plymouth Road looking east in 2003.*

Above: *A view of the town from Plymouth Road.* (RJ)

Above: *In February 1963, the Dousland to Princetown Road became passable for the first time in three weeks during the severe weather of that winter. A heavy crawler tractor dug a way through at Devil's Elbow, near Princetown.* (HC)

Left: *Plymouth Road, 1963.* (SA)

Inset left: *A high snowdrift in Plymouth Road, 1963.* (SA)

Left: *Grandfather Cooper (right) and a colleague.* (DG)

Below: *George Shillabeer (1797–1866) of Bellever. Inventor of the London omnibus, based on a Parisian bus, that ran from Paddington to the Bank. The cost was 1/- and it ran every three hours.* (DG)

Above: Left to right: *Doris Mather, Gran Cooper and Aunt Doris.* (DG)

Left: *Mr Faulkner.* (DG)

The bar at the Plume of Feathers before enlargement, early 1950s. Left to right: Fred Pengelly, Gib 'Jasper' Crocker (landlord), Joe Salter. (LC)

George Langton took over the pub on 20 March 1968 and altered it internally to enlarge the seating area. His wife, Pam, ran the business and successfully developed a great following of country music enthusiasts with the Pheasant-Pluckers and later the Porridge Group. Pam's health was not good and their son James retired from sea in 1974 to become a partner. After Pam died James took over the licence and extended the pub; he remains the landlord at the time of writing.

In 1808 the Duchy leased the land at **Plymouth Hill** to Edward Vosper and to John Watts, each of whom had a cottage and garden on the south side close to Princetown Square, and to Anthony Cooper and Richard Underhayes (who also had the stable) on the north side. Now, along its south side, Plymouth Hill is a terrace of houses which were built in 1912 and differ somewhat from those on the north side. Winnie Cooper (née Halfyard) has lived here for all of her 85 years in the house where she was born. Apart from upgrading the lavatory and bath, the property has not changed, although the Duchy did install a solid-fuel Rayburn in the early 1950s (it would be another half-century before gas would be brought to the town).

The two **Lodges** at the end of Plymouth Road are similar to those at Tor Royal and Beardown and were built by the Duchy in 1913 or 1914 to mark the estate boundaries and perhaps to house grooms for the Prince of Wales' horses.

From here the road leads over the moor to Yelverton. Devil's Bridge, spanning some old open-cast tin workings, was a particularly treacherous part of the journey and the road has been straightened out. Some 200 yards from the road is Double Waters, a pit where land-mines were detonated. Further to the south of the bridge is Hartor, an old rifle range.

Memorial to the Babb family in Princetown churchyard, south of the church.

The journey back to Princetown begins at the **North Lodge**. **Babbs Cottages** is a pair of semi-detached, slate-hung dwellings, one of which is owned at the time of writing by Anna Easton, daughter of George Langton. The cottages were designed by the Duchy architect, Mr Alexander. A detached house appears next and then another, **Hillside**. Following this the Duchy Hotel appears on the corner of Princetown Square.

The Devil's Elbow at Devil's Bridge. Unemployed men were paid a paltry sum of money per yard to crush stones for the roads. There are what appear to be concrete blocks in the tinners' gulley or gert, perhaps the remnants of military training or power line supports. (DG)

POSTSCRIPT

Those who explore Princetown and its surrounding area are likely to be surprised by the wealth of history to be discovered in the buildings and the landscape – as rich as that anywhere on the moor and in many ways more visible.

This grim little granite town... with its dark grey granite,
its prison, its radio and television masts, Princetown has
little to offer us... we would urge you to pass quickly by
in search of happier objectives.

(P.A. Titchmarsh, *Dartmoor County by Car*)

The many who explore this granite town with its neighbourhood do find its history all-absorbing. There is much to see here but the sights and sounds of the past, whether appreciated in briliant sunshine or the swirling mists of winter, are there to be enjoyed by all. Peter Alex Lambert's words in 2003 convey something of the sense of this unique town and neighbourhood:

Disembodied granite voices
Dream on
As morning mists lie sleeping
New growth shines
As old eyes watch through gorse and heather
Strong words in wild winds rejoicing.

Impatient rivers carry the words
Dancing through craggy tors and heather hills
Stormy clouds race high
Drifts of icy lace sparkle
On Dartmoor's bridal white
The spirit of the moor and its people
Joined in winter's rest.

(Alex Lambert, 2003)

SUBSCRIBERS

SUBSCRIBERS

Shirley Agness, Princetown, Devon
Margaret K. Atwill, Horrabridge, Devon
Mandy Bacon, Heddington, Wiltshire
Mr A.J. Berry, Horrabridge, Devon
Professor and Mrs J. Berry, Yelverton, Devon
The Revd David Bolt
Mr and Mrs M. Buller, Princetown, Devon
John and Sally Burchell, Princetown, Devon
K.J. Burrow, Bucks Cross, Devon
Sheila Coates, Princetown
Heather Collings, Penzance. Granddaughter of
    Dingley and Dot Bolt
Stephen Collings, Over Cambridge. Grandson
    of Dingley and Dot Bolt
Margaret Collings (née Bolt), daughter of
    Dingley Bolt of "Top Shop"
Major Michael Cooke, Plymouth, Devon
Bryan Cooper, Whitchurch, Tavistock
Mr David Cooper, Postbridge, Devon
Winnie Cooper, Princetown, Devon
C.H. Cooper, Tavistock, Devon
Rodney H. Cooper, Horrabridge, Devon
D.G.H. Cooper, Princetown, Devon
Brenda Cooper (née Cribbett), Whitchurch,
    Tavistock
Richard Cribbett, Plymouth
Mabel Cribbett, Princetown
Mavis and Allan Cross
Eric Cruse, Princetown, Devon
Miss R. Cundy, Lamerton, Devon
Mr B.G. Dingle, Tavistock, Devon
Jemma and Paul Doidge, Tavistock
Ruth Draper, Oxford. Granddaughter of
    Dingley and Dot Bolt
Gary Robert Easton, Princetown, Devon
Kevan J. Elliott, Princetown, Devon
Prof Alan E.H. Emery, Budleigh Salterton, Devon
Mr R. Evans, Boscombe, Bournemouth, Dorset
F.C. Evans, grandson of Samuel Worth
Dora Fallon, Princetown
John Foulkes, Dawlish, Devon
Irene E. Frampton
David E. German
B.R. Goulden, Glebe House, Higher Ashton,
    Exeter, Devon
Mrs A. Grigg, Two Bridge, Princetown
C. Heywood, Princetown
Peter Hirst, Dartmeet
Mr. Joy, Tavistock, Devon
Ron Joy, Tavistock, Devon
L. Claire Koczka (née Stephens), Dartmoor
    Garage, Princetown
Kathy Lake-Bullen, Tywyn, Gwynedd
George S. Langton, Princetown

Arthur and Anne Lowrey, Princetown, Devon
Donald Lye, Princetown, Devon
Patrick McQuillen, Burrator Avenue
Lt Col and Mrs R.A. Middleton, Yelverton, Devon
Doris and Bert Millgate, Maidstone, Kent
Derek H. Morgan, Dousland
Katrina and Shaun Oakes, Okehampton
Mr N.J. Osborne, Westbury, Wiltshire
Fred Owen, Princetown, Devon
Rosie Parker, Reading. Granddaughter of
    Dingley and Dot Bolt
David and Terri Parnall, Dousland, Yelverton,
    Devon
Kenneth C. Parnell, Totnes, Devon
Frances M. Pengelly
David Pengelly, Princetown, Devon
Mr and Mrs R.M. Perry, Plymouth, Devon
Mike and Sue Pesterfield, Tavistock, Devon
Plymouth College Library
Audrey Prizeman, Plymouth, Devon
Louis Rich, Princetown, Devon
Ken Rickard, Lydford, Devon
Kimberley and Adrian Roderick, Princetown,
    Devon
Mr and Mrs Rolfe, Lower Dimson, Cornwall
Rosemary and Derek Roper, Yelverton, Devon
Peter Saunders, Ringwood, Hampshire
Mr F.L. and Mrs P.J. Shelton, South Wingfield,
    Derbyshire
William J. Short, Two Bridges, Princetown
Mr W.J. Steele, Princetown
Les Stephens, Tavistock, Devon
Rosemary M. Stephens, formerly of Princetown
The Family Stones, Princetown
Graham Thorne, Maldon, Essex
Anne Trask, Dawlish, Devon
The Two Bridges Hotel
Mr and Mrs R.A. Vane, Lincoln
F.E. Vernon, The Pines, Honiton, Devon
Mr G. Waldron, Plymouth, Devon
R.W. Walker, Princetown, Devon
Donald Warne, Tiverton
Mr and Mrs K. Watts, Princetown, Devon
John Waycott, Dousland, Yelverton, Devon
Peter Weatherly
Reverend John W.M. Weir
Dave J. Westwood, Princetown
Mr P.D. Whitcomb, Salisbury, Wiltshire
Gladys Williams, Princetown, Devon
George Williams
Andrew P. Young, Princetown, Devon
Adrian E. Young, Princetown, Devon
Sarah Youngson
Zenta, Ray, Hana and Fern Zubka-Hill,
    Yelverton, West Devon

Community Histories

The Book of Addiscombe • Canning & Clyde Road Residents
Association & Friends
The Book of Addiscombe, Vol. II • Canning & Clyde Road
Residents Association & Friends
The Book of Axminster with Kilmington • Les Berry
and Gerald Gosling
The Book of Bampton • Caroline Seward
The Book of Barnstaple • Avril Stone
The Book of Barnstaple, Vol. II • Avril Stone
The Book of The Bedwyns • The Bedwyn History Society
The Book of Bickington • Stuart Hands
Blandford Forum: A Millennium Portrait • Blandford Town Council
The Book of Bramford • Bramford Local History Group
The Book of Breage & Germoe • Stephen Polglase
The Book of Bridestowe • R. Cann
The Book of Bridport • Rodney Legg
The Book of Brixham • Frank Pearce
The Book of Buckfastleigh • Sandra Coleman
The Book of Buckland Monachorum & Yelverton • Hemery
The Book of Carharrack • Carharrack Old Cornwall Society
The Book of Carshalton • Stella Wilks and Gordon Rookledge
The Parish Book of Cerne Abbas • Vale and Vale
The Book of Chagford • Ian Rice
The Book of Chapel-en-le-Frith • Mike Smith
The Book of Chittlehamholt with
Warkleigh & Satterleigh • Richard Lethbridge
The Book of Chittlehampton • Various
The Book of Colney Heath • Bryan Lilley
The Book of Constantine • Moore and Trethowan
The Book of Cornwood & Lutton • Compiled by the People of
the Parish
The Book of Creech St Michael • June Small
The Book of Cullompton • Compiled by the People of the Parish
The Book of Dawlish • Frank Pearce
The Book of Dulverton, Brushford,
Bury & Exebridge • Dulverton & District Civic Society
The Book of Dunster • Hilary Binding
The Book of Edale • Gordon Miller
The Ellacombe Book • Sydney R. Langmead
The Book of Exmouth • W.H. Pascoe
The Book of Grampound with Creed • Bane and Oliver
The Book of Hayling Island & Langstone • Rogers
The Book of Helston • Jenkin with Carter
The Book of Hemyock • Clist and Dracott
The Book of Herne Hill • Patricia Jenkyns
The Book of Hethersett • Hethersett Society Research Group
The Book of High Bickington • Avril Stone
The Book of Ilsington • Dick Wills
The Book of Kingskerswell • Carsewella Local History Group
The Book of Lamerton • Ann Cole & Friends
Lanner, A Cornish Mining Parish • Sharron
Schwartz and Roger Parker
The Book of Leigh & Bransford • Malcolm Scott
The Book of Litcham with Lexham & Mileham • Litcham Historical
& Amenity Society
The Book of Loddiswell • Reg and Betty Sampson
The New Book of Lostwithiel • Barbara Fraser
The Book of Lulworth • Rodney Legg
The Book of Lustleigh • Joe Crowdy
The Book of Lyme Regis • Rodney Legg
The Book of Manaton • Compiled by the People of the Parish
The Book of Markyate • Markyate Local History Society

The Book of Mawnan • Mawnan Local History Group
The Book of Meavy • Pauline Hemery
The Book of Minehead with Alcombe • Binding and Stevens
The Book of Morchard Bishop • Jeff Kingaby
The Book of Newdigate • John Callcut
The Book of Nidderdale • Nidderdale Musuem Society
The Book of Northlew with Ashbury • Northlew History Group
The Book of North Newton • Robins and Robins
The Book of North Tawton • Baker, Hoare and Shields
The Book of Nynehead • Nynehead & District History Society
The Book of Okehampton • Radford and Radford
The Book of Paignton • Frank Pearce
The Book of Penge, Anerley & Crystal Palace • Peter Abbott
The Book of Peter Tavy with Cudlipptown • Peter Tavy
Heritage Group
The Book of Pimperne • Jean Coull
The Book of Plymtree • Tony Eames
The Book of Porlock • Denis Corner
Postbridge – The Heart of Dartmoor • Reg Bellamy
The Book of Priddy • Albert Thompson
The Book of Princetown • Dr Gardner-Thorpe
The Book of Rattery • By the People of the Parish
The Book of St Day • Joseph Mills and Paul Annear
The Book of Sampford Courtenay
with Honeychurch • Stephanie Pouya
The Book of Sculthorpe • Gary Windeler
The Book of Seaton • Ted Gosling
The Book of Sidmouth • Ted Gosling and Sheila Luxton
The Book of Silverton • Silverton Local History Society
The Book of South Molton • Jonathan Edmunds
The Book of South Stoke with Midford • Edited by Robert Parfitt
South Tawton & South Zeal with Sticklepath • Radfords
The Book of Sparkwell with Hemerdon & Lee Mill • Pam James
The Book of Staverton • Pete Lavis
The Book of Stithians • Stithians Parish History Group
The Book of Stogumber, Monksilver, Nettlecombe
& Elworthy • Maurice and Joyce Chidgey
The Book of Studland • Rodney Legg
The Book of Swanage • Rodney Legg
The Book of Tavistock • Gerry Woodcock
The Book of Thorley • Sylvia McDonald and Bill Hardy
The Book of Torbay • Frank Pearce
Uncle Tom Cobley & All:
Widecombe-in-the-Moor • Stephen Woods
The Book of Watchet • Compiled by David Banks
The Book of West Huntspill • By the People of the Parish
Widecombe-in-the-Moor • Stephen Woods
The Book of Williton • Michael Williams
The Book of Witheridge • Peter and Freda Tout and John Usmar
The Book of Withycombe • Chris Boyles
Woodbury: The Twentieth Century Revisited • Roger Stokes
The Book of Woolmer Green • Compiled by the People of the Parish

For details of any of the above titles or if you are
interested in writing your own history, please contact:
Commissioning Editor Community Histories, Halsgrove House,
Lower Moor Way, Tiverton Business Park, Tiverton, Devon EX16
6SS, England; email: naomic@halsgrove.com

In order to include as many historical photographs as possible in this volume, a printed index is not included. However, the Devon titles in the Community History Series are indexed by Genuki. For further information and indexes to various volumes in the series, please visit: http://www.cs.ncl.ac.uk/genuki/DEV/indexingproject.html